THE SENATE OF CANADA

UNDERSTANDING CANADA

THE SENATE OF CANADA

Gary William O'Brien

UNIVERSITY OF TORONTO PRESS
Toronto Buffalo London

INSTITUTE OF PARLIAMENTARY AND POLITICAL LAW
INSTITUT DE DROIT PARLEMENTAIRE ET POLITIQUE

© University of Toronto Press 2023

Irwin Law

An imprint of University of Toronto Press

Toronto Buffalo London

utorontopress.com

Printed and bound by CPI Group (UK) Ltd, Croydon, CR0 4YY

ISBN 978-1-5522-1657-6 (paper)   ISBN 978-1-5522-1658-3 (PDF)

Library and Archives Canada Cataloguing in Publication

Title: The senate of Canada / Gary William O'Brien.

Names: O'Brien, Gary William, author.

Description: Series statement: Understanding Canada collection | Includes bibliographical references and index.

Identifiers: Canadiana (print) 2023020886X | Canadiana (ebook) 20230208959 | ISBN 9781552216576 (softcover) | ISBN 9781552216583 (PDF)

Subjects: LCSH: Canada. Parliament. Senate.

Classification: LCC JL155 .O35 2023 | DDC 328.71071—dc23

Cover image: Adobe Stock

We wish to acknowledge the land on which the University of Toronto Press operates. This land is the traditional territory of the Wendat, the Anishnaabeg, the Haudenosaunee, the Métis, and the Mississaugas of the Credit First Nation. University of Toronto Press acknowledges the financial support of the Government of Canada and the Ontario Arts Council, an agency of the Government of Ontario, for its publishing activities.

2 3 4 5   27 26 25 24

To the former Speakers

Dan Hays, Noël Kinsella, and the late Gildas Molgat:

Three giants of the Senate

Contents

Foreword

The term "senate" was first applied to an assembly of elders who had tasks of advising the ultimate holder of power in ancient Rome. After a long hiatus, the notion of senate resurfaced in European states such as the United Kingdom during the Age of Enlightenment. In its more modern interpretation, the designation has come to mean a parliamentary body based, in principle, on the nobility or "first estate," or a chamber of wise thought aiming to rectify the political interests and excesses of the lower house of Parliament. In countries with extensive and difficult geography, like Canada, a senate was also thought of as having a role in providing a voice for distant and less densely populated areas. It was into this historical soil that, in 1867, the *British North America Act*, now called the *Constitution Act, 1867*, planted a living tree in Canada capable of growth and expansion within its natural limits. The Senate of Canada was, and continues to be, a major branch of that living tree.

The specific model for the Senate of Canada was the United Kingdom's House of Lords, as far as circumstances would permit. Since Confederation, the two institutions have developed in different directions. While the Senate of this country may today still appear somewhat similar in principle to its British forebear, over the 155 years of Confederation it has developed into a unique parliamentary institution. Today, the Senate of Canada is enshrined both in the text of the Constitution and in statute law. Further, it is deeply embedded in constitutional custom and convention, partly through law as well as in policy. Various aspects of the structure and functioning of the Senate are also examined and explained in decisions of the Supreme Court. Most significantly, that Court affirmed a few years ago that as part of the core fabric of Canada's architecture, the Senate could not be dispensed with, or significantly altered, without the unanimous agreement of both Canada and the jurisdictions that form part of it.

Beyond the Constitution, the law, and the policies that are encrusted around it, the upper house of the Parliament of Canada plays a vital role in the political life of the country. The Senate reads, indeed on occasion amends, legislation enacted by the House of Commons. It originates studies into topics of currency in government and society. Through its focus on the regions of Canada, it balances the "representation by population" characteristic of the lower house. For all these reasons, the study of Canada that omits the Senate is necessarily incomplete.

Gary O'Brien is uniquely placed to offer this study. He holds a PhD in political science from Carleton University, where his dissertation focused on the legislative and parliamentary practices of pre-Confederation Canada. As the twelfth clerk of the Senate, for the years 2009–2015, and as a continuing Senate scholar, he is familiar with the history of the institution, with its function in Canadian parliamentary and political life, as well as with its functioning. This book is a reflection of his experience and expertise.

Gregory Tardi, DJur
Editor, Understanding Canada Collection
January 2022

CHAPTER ONE

What Is the Senate?

The Senate of Canada is the upper house of the Parliament of Canada. As one scholar has observed, it is "a uniquely Canadian institution to serve uniquely Canadian needs."[1] It is composed of 105 appointed members who represent the various provinces and territories of the country. The distribution of seats is made on a regional basis, with twenty-four senators from the Maritimes Division, twenty-four from the Quebec Division, twenty-four from the Ontario Division, and twenty-four from the Western Division. The Province of Newfoundland and Labrador has six senators, and the three territories (Yukon, the Northwest Territories, and Nunavut) have one senator each.

The Canadian Senate is the only non-elected legislature in Canada and its only upper house.[2] Senators are summoned by the Governor General on the advice of the prime minister and can serve until the age of seventy-five. Despite its non-elective basis, the Senate's legislative powers are identical to those of the House of Commons with two exceptions: money bills must originate in the House of Commons; and amendments to the Canadian Constitution can be made without the agreement of the Senate.[3]

There have been only a few constitutional amendments affecting the Senate. A mandatory retirement age of seventy-five was adopted in 1965, and a 180-day suspensive veto on constitutional amendments was made statutory in 1982. Also in 1982, it was agreed that the powers of the Senate, the method of selecting senators, and the number of senators per province would be subject to the general amending provision requiring support in seven provinces that have at least 50 percent of the population. The Constitution has also been amended to add new senators as the number of provinces and territories increase.

Despite its unelected foundation, the Senate is an intrinsic part of the parliamentary process. The Supreme Court has stated that "the Senate is one of Canada's foundational political institutions. It lies at the heart of the agreements that gave birth to the Canadian federation."[4] George Brown, one of the Fathers of Confederation, told the members of his party at the time of Confederation:

> that no opposition on their part ought to be offered to the creation of a Senate as an integral part of the Constitution of this country; that it was the price of representation by population, that it was part of the bargain, and that it ought to be accepted.[5]

Its original purpose was to bring the very large and dispersed colonial provinces of British North America together and be a unifying force within the new Dominion. As Brown said, "on no other condition" — agreement on the Senate — "could we have advanced a step."[6]

Among contemporary upper chambers, the Senate is one of the most powerful. In a paper presented to the British House of Commons in 2007, Jack Straw, the Government Leader of the House and Lord Privy Seal, described Canada's upper house as follows:

> On the face of it, one of the most powerful second chambers in the world is the wholly appointed Canadian Senate. When the Canadian Parliament was established, the Senate's powers were based on those of the pre-1911 House of Lords. Even today, Canada has no equivalent of the Parliament Acts. There are only two restrictions on the Senate's nominal powers: financial legislation must be introduced in the first chamber; and, although the Senate may amend financial legislation, it cannot increase taxation.[7]

Prime Minister Wilfrid Laurier grasped the enormity of the Senate's legislative powers when he told the House of Commons in 1908:

> But if under our constitution in Canada there was a deadlock between the House of Commons and the Senate, nothing short of revolution could solve the difficulty … no constitutional remedy within our grasp could bring the Senate to a different view.[8]

Historically, the membership of the Senate has included Canadians with distinguished achievements and varied backgrounds.[9] Two prime ministers have sat in the Senate: Sir John Abbott (1891–1892) and Sir Mackenzie Bowell (1894–1896). Appointments often represented Canada's social diversity. The first woman to be appointed was Cairine Reay Mackay Wilson in 1930.[10] The first senator of Indigenous birth was James Gladstone in 1958, two years before the federal franchise was extended to Indigenous peoples living on reserves.

The investigative work undertaken by its committees is considered of great quality, and indeed of a higher standard than that of the House of Commons.[11] Its reports have received international recognition. For example, in 1971, an American congressman, Charles Mosher, claimed the four-volume report on science policy produced by a special committee chaired by Senator Maurice Lamontagne was "the most thorough study of any in the world."[12]

Yet it is an institution that has never been fully accepted into the Canadian political system. Few observers ever recommend its design to other countries. Writing in 2002, David C Docherty observed that the Canadian Senate "represents and embodies some of the most anti-democratic features of representative assemblies … [I]t ranks as one of the last reformed chambers in Westminster-based parliamentary democracies."[13] CES Franks saw the Senate's chief characteristic as not what it does but that it has survived. He declared the Senate to be a "frustrating puzzle."[14] Others have described the Senate as being "simply a fifth wheel on the governmental coach"[15] and a "political conundrum,"[16] which poses for Canadians "a democratic dilemma."[17]

In the first major academic study of the Senate, Robert A Mackay entitled his opening chapter "The Problem" and his last chapter "To End or Mend the Senate?"[18] The Co-operative Commonwealth Federation's (CCF) *Regina Manifesto* of 1933 called for the abolition of the Senate, a position Canada's New Democratic Party has repeatedly taken. Its improvement is the subject of numerous books and articles. David E Smith has written: "Few studies of the Senate do not talk about, if they are not devoted to, its reform. Indeed, 'Reform of the Senate' must be one of the hoariest topics in Canadian politics."[19]

Notwithstanding the Senate's vast bibliography, it is an institution often misunderstood,[20] and since, as the saying goes, "misunderstanding breeds distrust," the concept of good governance demands this mistrust be addressed. The purpose of this book is to help us better understand the Senate as a national institution in hopes that a more informed debate on Canada's system of parliamentary government can take place. We will examine how the Senate came to be, what it does, how it compares with other second chambers, how it functions, and what the prospects for structural reform are.

In two judicial opinions, the Supreme Court of Canada has described the Senate as having a "fundamental nature and role."[21] We need therefore to explore what that "fundamental nature and role" is, since "nature" is not a term that can be simply defined by positive law. As the ancient philosophers taught us, "Nature, however understood, is not known by nature. Nature had to be discovered."[22]

Two of the problems in studying the Senate are a tendency to read the present into the past in the hope of justifying the Senate's current actions, and being selective in the evidence about how the Fathers of Confederation saw the Senate's purpose. For example, we cannot discern the totality of the views of Canada's first prime minister, Sir John A Macdonald, by simply examining the minutes of the 1864 Quebec Conference. We must also look at his differing remarks during the *Confederation Debates* when the seventy-two resolutions were ratified by the legislature of the Province of Canada.

Another problem is the temptation to examine the Senate from an *a priori* perspective. Some dislike the fact that the Senate is not elected, while others resent it may not be representative of the average Canadian. Such inquiries can lead to bias.

This study will approach the Senate more conceptually, namely through the prism of bicameralism. Bicameral institutions are legislative bodies whose deliberations involve two distinct assemblies. The essence of the Parliament of Canada is that it is bicameral, consisting of the Senate and the House of Commons. The British essayist Walter Bagehot once remarked with respect to the British parliamentary system, "if we had an ideal House of Commons … it is certain we should not need a higher Chamber."[23] The Senate's composition, its powers, and its functions are always linked to the bicameral process, which, as we will later discuss, poses problems for its reform.

Chapter 2 will review the various theories and structures of bicameralism, while Chapter 3 will attempt to show how those models were adapted to Canadian realities. Janet Ajzenstat writes that the Fathers were no strangers to political theory. They were, above all, thinkers about their country and about politics:

> The Fathers of Confederation and Canada's founding legislators exhibited an impressive knowledge of constitutional history and theoretical texts. They cited British, American, and French authorities, studied European constitutions, and compared federal systems … some at least knew Thomas Hobbes, John Locke, Montesquieu and Rousseau. Mill's *Representative Government*, published in 1861, is the most often-cited book. Many had read the famous documents of US constitutional history, especially the *Federalist Papers*. They referred to sections of the American Constitution and to constitutions of the individual states.[24]

In Chapter 4, we will look at the roles the Senate has historically played regarding federalism, parliamentary government, and the review of legislation. Applying the various models of bicameralism that compose the Senate's design will help us better evaluate how well the Senate has fulfilled its constitutional duties.

Chapter 5 will provide a snapshot of the Senate as a parliamentary institution, specifically its most salient features and procedures. Chapter 6 will focus on examples of the Senate at work. Four case studies will be reviewed: (1) its examination of *An Act to amend the Patent Act* in 1987; (2) the Pearson Airport inquiry of 1992; (3) the Special Senate Committee on Poverty (the Croll inquiry, 1969 to 1971); and (4) the Special Committee on the Cape Breton Development Corporation of 1996.

In 2015, with the election of the Liberal government of Justin Trudeau, an effort was made to revive Canadian bicameralism by creating a Senate composed of non-partisan legislators who would use influence as opposed to political power when they engaged with the House of Commons. Chapter 7 will focus on this new non-partisan, complementary Senate and its workways. The final chapter will review past proposals for reform and the impediments they faced, as well as the prospects of achieving structural change to the Senate's design.

As Canada moves more deeply into the twenty-first century, the challenges of parliamentary government will not lessen. The capacity of Parliament to effectively deal with those challenges will be stronger if Canadians accept and value the contribution of their bicameral system. It is therefore essential that there be a better understanding of Parliament's upper house, the role it plays in governance, and how that role can be improved.

Second Chambers — Theories and Structures

Bicameralism is described as of one of the great forms of government. Laurence Sterne notes the ancient Germans had the wise custom of debating everything of importance to their state twice: once when drunk, and once when sober: "drunk — that their councils might not want vigour; and sober — that they might not want discretion."[1] Its origins can be traced to classical times, as well as to the idea of the "balanced constitution" embodied in the Glorious Revolution of 1688. Janet Ajzenstat believes "it remains a fact that the parliamentary system of checks and balances, with bicameralism at its heart, is the world's greatest political invention."[2]

"Bicameralism" encompasses ideas and structures. It is essentially a constitutional principle by which power is legally divided. Bicameral legislative institutions are those whose deliberations involve two assemblies. It is distinguished from "unicameralism" by which legislative decisions are taken by a single chamber.

The debate as to whether a political system should have one or two assemblies is centuries old. The Greek and Roman philosophers argued the merits of having "mixed" or "simple" government. The most influential proponent of bicameralism was Polybius, who felt the strength of Rome lay in its mixed constitution, in which the elements — the Consuls, the Senate, and the popular assemblies —

were in exact equilibrium. Professor Sabine writes: "Polybius thus gave to mixed government the form of a system of checks and balances, the form in which it passed to Montesquieu and the founders of the American constitution."[3]

In more modern times, as the call for democracy grew stronger, the principle of bicameralism versus unicameralism was passionately debated. John Adams, in *Thoughts on Government* (1776), opposed unicameralism, believing that a single chamber was liable to all the vices and frailties of an individual, such as making hasty and absurd judgments, and acting in his own self interest. Tom Paine, the author of *The Rights of Man* (1791), felt that a freely elected single chamber like France's National Assembly was the only one needed since it represented "enlightened mankind" and showed "the proper character of man."[4] The controversy over bicameralism versus unicameralism continues today. The abolition of the House of Lords is still a salient issue in contemporary British politics, as well as in Canada.

The Models of Bicameralism

Modern bicameralism embraces varying ideas or rationales. Nolte and Llanos describe these as follows: (1) representation of different interests; (2) preservation of liberties and individual rights; (3) improvement of the quality of legislation; and (4) the stability of legislative outcomes. They write:

> The underlying idea was, that the interests of each estate could only be protected by the mutual veto of the chambers. Nowadays, the idea of reserving one legislative chamber for the nobles has lost legitimacy, but what did survive was the idea of using two chambers to accommodate different political, economic or social interests, and in so doing, to promote the enactment of legislation based on a greater social and political consensus.[5]

Bicameralism can be better understood by using classification models. Such models are analytical concepts that explore the ideas of power and representation within their political contexts. Bicameral theory identifies at least four such models: (1) *the mixed government model*, which is based on the premise that the branches of government balance each other to ensure one is not the master of any other; (2) the non-competitive and deferential model, which describes the actions of second chambers toward the popularly elected house within the context of modern democratic government — it can also be referred to as *the complementary model*; (3) *the territorial model*, which focuses on representation of citizens from a regional and local level and supplements national representation in the lower house; and (4) *the popular sovereignty model*, wherein the members of the upper house are selected by "the people." The theoretical objectives and origins of these models are described below.

The Mixed Government Model

According to this model, the upper house provides a balance between the executive and the lower house and a mutual check. It is essentially a political model since it deals with the power relationships between the two legislative chambers.

The justification of a "balanced constitution" in seventeenth-century England rested on the belief that having three independent and competing authorities — the King, Lords, and Commons — was the mark of a free state.[6] Without it, anarchy would follow. In what is perhaps the first constitutional description of the theory of mixed government, namely *Charles I's Answer to the Nineteen Propositions* (1641), the role of the House of Lords is described as follows:

> In this Kingdom the Laws are jointly made by a King, by a House
> of Peers, and by a House of Commons chosen by the People, all
> having free Votes and particular Priviledges ... And the Lords,
> being entrusted with a Judicatory Power, are an excellent Skreen
> and Bank between the Prince and People, to assist each against any
> Incroachments of the other; and by just Judgments to preserve
> that Law, which ought to be the Rule of every one of the Three.[7]

The idea that mixed government protected liberty was further added to by Charles-Louis Montesquieu and John Stuart Mill. Montesquieu, in *The Spirit of the Laws* (1748), believed that to safeguard liberty, each legislative house must be a check on the other. It was able to accomplish this "by the mutual privilege of refusing."[8] Mill, in *Considerations on Representative Government* (1861), made this statement of why a second house is needed as a protection of liberty from despotism:

> The consideration which tells most, in my judgment, in favour of two Chambers … is the evil effect produced upon the mind of any holder of power, whether an individual or an assembly, by the consciousness of having only themselves to consult. It is important that no set of persons should, in great affairs, be able, even temporarily, to make their sic volo prevail without asking any one else for his consent. A majority in a single assembly, when it has assumed a permanent character — when composed of the same persons habitually acting together, and always assured of victory in their own House — easily becomes despotic and overweening, if released from the necessity of considering whether its acts will be concurred in by another constituted authority.[9]

The Complementary Model

In countries that have popularly elected lower houses, appointed second chambers can provide "efficient, apolitical functions."[10] Philip Norton, a professor of government and member of the House of Lords, gives perhaps the best description of the complementary model. The Lords' activities "derive from the House's seeking to complement and not challenge the work of the elected chamber. The House seeks to add value to the political process." Its contribution is one of reflection, not competition.[11]

With the rise of democracy and the adoption of the *Representation of the People Act* (the 1832 Reform Bill), the House of Commons emerged as the focal point of parliamentary government. Pursuant to the *Parliament Act 1911*, the House of Lords would henceforth have only a suspensive veto over legislation. While the Lords would still be included in the tripart division of power, the conventions of Parliament would change so that the upper house would become non-threatening. Its primary focus was not to check but to influence the elected house by exhibiting greater experience, memory, and knowledge of legislative matters. By putting forward authority and expertise, as opposed to "killer amendments," appointed complementary chambers could play a more relevant role in modern legislative decision making.

The Territorial Model

A third model of bicameralism focuses on representation. It is particularly relevant to large, diverse countries as it gives second chambers the opportunity to represent territorial concerns in national institutions and counter majority rule.[12] It is primarily an American innovation. The "Great Compromise" of the Constitutional Convention held in Philadelphia in 1787 was that the House of Representatives would be elected according to population while the Senate would have equal representation for each state. In *The Federalist Papers*, James Madison wrote: "A government founded on principles more consonant to the wishes of the larger States is not likely to be obtained from the smaller States."[13] While the lower chamber would reflect the popular dimension of politics, the upper chamber would represent territorial diversity and bring a broader consensus to adopted legislation.

Over time, the territorial model has been revised to provide for the protection of minorities not located in one specific geographical area, for example, through the selection of members from linguistic communities, as in Belgium, or religious minorities, as in Bosnia and Herzegovina.[14]

The Popular Sovereignty Model

A fourth model of bicameralism also emphasizes representation. Through the democratic selection of representatives to two legislative houses, the executive will be more effectively controlled. As Lord Campion, a former clerk of the British House of Commons, observed, in order to stand up to the popular house on behalf of minorities, "a Second House was found to need a democratic basis which could only be secured by some form of popular election."[15]

The popular sovereignty model is founded on the principle that the people's view can find greater expression if two chambers are elected. By doing so, more opportunity will be given to smaller political parties and independents to have a voice in national decision making. The model is often characterized by each house using a different electoral process to select members, for example, simple majorities in one house and a form of proportional representation in the other. To avoid legislative deadlock, a conflict resolution mechanism needs to be formulated. Without such agreement, it will be difficult for a legislature to operate efficiently.[16]

Theory Versus Practice: A Cautionary Note

While theory can justify two house arrangements, it cannot claim credit for the creation or functioning of a state's bicameral system. Each institution's architecture is subject to the wisdom of "cutting the shoe to fit the foot." What model a country chooses is usually determined by its political and historical roots. Meg Russell writes:

> [W]hich model is the most effective or desirable? The answer to a large extent will be culturally specific: it depends on the benefits that a country seeks from its bicameral arrangements, as well as the way in which these arrangements work in practice. This in turn is fundamentally connected to factors such as history and tradition, the territorial structure and party system.[17]

The theory and practice of bicameral models may at times be contradictory. For example, in the United Kingdom, the "complementary" House of Lords has a history of causing majority governments serious headaches. Harold Wilson's administration was often frustrated by the Lords, as was Edward Heath's. Margaret Thatcher's government also experienced resistance. The clash over the *War Crimes Act*, introduced in 1990, could only be resolved by invoking the *Parliament Act*, which allowed a bill to become law without the Lords' consent. Thatcher's large majorities in the Commons encouraged the Lords' boldness, as some sensed legislation would pass too quickly without proper scrutiny.[18]

It should also be noted that many upper houses have a mixed composition. The Spanish *Senado* consists mostly of directly elected members, but also includes indirectly elected members, selected by the legislative assemblies of autonomous communities. While most Italian senators are elected, a small number are non-elected. The majority of members of Belgium's upper house are elected, but there are also members indirectly elected, appointed, or hereditary.[19]

The Structure of Second Chambers

According to data compiled by the Inter-Parliamentary Union in 2021, of the 192 national parliaments in the world, 81 (42 percent) are bicameral while 111 (58 percent) are unicameral.[20] Larger countries tend to have bicameral parliaments. For example, the United States, Russia, India, Pakistan, Australia, Brazil, and South Africa all have two-house legislatures. Most Western European countries — the United Kingdom, Ireland, France, Germany, Italy, and Spain — practise bicameralism. Countries that have federal constitutions tend to be bicameral.

Regarding the selection of members, close to half of the world's Senates use the popular sovereignty model — that is, they are elected, either directly or indirectly. The United States, Italy, Mexico, and the Philippines have wholly directly elected second chambers. Pakistan's upper house is wholly indirectly elected while India's *Rajya*

Sabha is majority indirectly elected and minority appointed. States with parliamentary systems and directly elected second chambers include Australia, the Czech Republic, and Japan. Other parliamentary systems, such as Austria and South Africa, have second chambers that are indirectly elected.[21]

Selection methods also include appointment. In many Caribbean countries (for example, the Bahamas, Barbados, Jamaica, and Trinidad and Tobago), senators are chosen by the Governor General. In the German *Bundesrat*, members are appointed by state governments to represent regional interests. The House of Lords has a mixed membership of hereditary peers, bishops, and life peers. Tsebelis and Money write that selection by appointment "may be based on outstanding performance or service to government or to a particular profession, recalling the Roman model of wise legislators seasoned by experience and age."[22]

Regarding institutional power, most second chambers are subordinate to the first chamber. Arend Lijphart notes:

> [T]heir negative votes on proposed legislation can often be overridden by the first chambers, and in parliamentary systems the cabinet is usually responsible primarily or exclusively to the first chamber ... The only fully symmetrical bicameral legislatures — those in which the two chambers are coequal in power — are (the United States, Italy, Belgium, and Switzerland) that have chambers with formally equal powers. The vast majority of the members of these four second chambers are also directly elected.[23]

Lijphart categorizes the Australian Senate as "moderately asymmetrical."[24] Its constitution provides for an elected House of Representatives and an elected Senate. Senate members are elected for six-year terms, with half the state senators standing for election every three years.[25]

Regarding territorial models, there are numerous examples. They appear in federal systems such as Austria, Germany, India, Mexico, Switzerland, and the United States, as well as in unitary nations, such as Spain. Venezuela provides for a degree of ethnic representation in its upper house, while Belgium ensures that lin-guistic communities are represented in its second chamber.[26]

The foregoing provides context by which to study our own upper house, the Senate of Canada. While the comparative study of second chamber design is instructive, the wisdom of "cutting the shoe to fit the foot" remains paramount. What the Fathers of Confederation took from bicameral theory and how they adapted it to Canadian realities is the subject of our next chapter.

CHAPTER THREE

The Vision of the Fathers

The movement toward Confederation can be dated from the announcement made by Governor General Edmund Head on 16 August 1858: that the Province of Canada, comprising Canada East (Quebec) and Canada West (Ontario), was ready to open unification discussions with the Imperial and Maritime governments. It took a few more years before the "Great Coalition" of George Brown and John A Macdonald was formed, which soon led to the attendance of representatives of central Canada at the Maritime governments' "Constitutional Conference" held at Charlottetown, Prince Edward Island, in September 1864.[1]

Following a meeting in Halifax, the delegates met again in October, this time in Quebec City, in what has been called "the meeting that made Canada."[2] The results of the Quebec Conference, known as the "Seventy-Two Resolutions," were widely published, discussed, and ratified following vigorous debates in the various colonial legislatures.[3] A further conference was held, this time in London, England, with the Imperial government in December 1866. The provisions of the Canadian Constitution were then enacted by the British Parliament as the *British North America Act* (now called the *Constitution Act, 1867*) on 29 March 1867.[4] The Dominion of Canada came into being on 1 July 1867.

There was little question the national government would require a bicameral Parliament. Danielle Pinard says it "was taken for granted."[5] British North America, divided by race, language, religion, and geographical distance, would clearly need a second chamber, but the question as to its role and structure remained to be determined.

The Senate was the pivotal question of the Quebec Conference, as nearly six of the fourteen days of discussion were devoted to how it would be constituted. The distribution of Senate seats was so hotly debated that at the conclusion of the fifth day, one newspaperman, Edward Whelan, "feared the collapse of the conference was imminent."[6] The Senate was key to unifying the new Dominion. George Brown would later declare that agreement on the Senate was an essential component of the compact:

> Our Lower Canadian friends have agreed to give us representation by population in the Lower House, on the express condition that they shall have equality in the Upper House. On no other condition could we have advanced a step.[7]

The Fathers' Vision

The Fathers of Confederation were guided by four important precepts. The first was political theory. As previously noted, they were no strangers to constitutional history or theories of bicameralism. A form of mixed government had been prescribed by the Imperial government for the British North American colonies since their earliest days. In the 1850s, some pre-Confederation legislatures experimented with the popular sovereignty model by electing their second house.[8] However, no one bicameral model had broad support.

The mixed government model, while bringing improvements to legislative proposals, had shown little independence from the executive and had not contributed to stable government. In 1834, the House of Assembly of Lower Canada (Quebec), in its Ninety-Two Resolutions, condemned the appointed Legislative Council as "the most powerful and most frequent cause of abuses of power, — of the infractions of the laws, — of the waste of the public revenue and property."[9] The political turmoil caused by the upper houses acting as unelected checks led in large part to the rebellions in Upper and Lower Canada in the late 1830s.

With the coming of responsible government, the co-equal power arrangement of mixed government needed redefining. Ministries, to stay in power, now only required the confidence of the lower assembly. Some, like Robert Baldwin,[10] believed the work of the second chamber should be confined to complementing that of the first. Baldwin felt second chambers still had an important role to play. In 1836, he wrote to Colonial Secretary Lord Glenelg, saying "it may in addition be urged that a second chamber of some kind has, at least in modern constitutional legislation, been deemed essential to good Government."[11]

Likewise, many found the elective upper chambers unsatisfactory. Following the Charlottetown Conference, New Brunswick Lieutenant Governor AH Gordon had written "with hardly an exception the elective principle as applied to the Legislative Council was decidedly condemned."[12] David E Smith identifies the criticisms levelled at the elected Legislative Council in central Canada, namely, the geographically large constituencies, the costs for candidates, and the potential for conflict with the lower house.[13] Colin Grittner writes the large property qualification "had drastically limited the pool of potential Councillors. While some constituencies held spirited elections, by 1864, a full two-thirds of Council seats went uncontested."[14]

George Brown had always opposed the popular sovereignty model. He felt an elected second house would "bring to a stop the machinery of government," cause deadlock, and was anti-parliamentary. During the 1855 debate on the bill to make the Legislative Council elected, Brown declared he wanted "no new checks on the force of public opinion."[15] In the *Confederation Debates* he stated:

> I have always been opposed to a second elective chamber, and I am so still, from the conviction that two elective houses are inconsistent with the right working of the British parliamentary

system. I voted, almost alone, against the change when the Council was made elective, but I have lived to see a vast majority of those who did the deed wish it had not been done.[16]

The Fathers were also cognizant of the American territorial model of second chambers and its recognition of the federal principle. That an upper house could act as a shield for regional representation, as well as an indirect protection for the French-speaking nationality of Lower Canada (Quebec), was not lost upon them. However, the American version was generally opposed. Given that their southern neighbour was enthralled in a terrible civil war, the Fathers were preoccupied with the threat of state sovereignty.[17] Permitting local governments to exclusively select senators to the national government was unappealing. As well, the US Senate was hardly an example of national unity.

A second precept was the importance of pragmatism if Canada was to remain stable and grow successfully. Almost all the Fathers of Confederation were experienced politicians who had played leading roles as their provinces evolved from pioneer societies into agricultural–commercial ones. Twenty years before, in his famous *Report*,[18] Lord Durham had described the pre-Confederation era as two nations "warring in the bosom of a single state." The Fathers grasped that political relationships needed to change. Confederation was achievable only if there was compromise on all sides. As a former Speaker of the Senate, Senator Pierre Claude Nolin later wrote: "The story of our development as a country, and the parallel evolution of our parliamentary institutions, is a story of pragmatic accommodation through adaptation and innovation."[19]

Thirdly, they recognized there was no need to build parliamentary institutions *de novo*. By 1867, there had been over a century of parliamentary government in British North America.[20] Its classic design combined an elected lower house with an appointed Legislative Council. The procedure for resolving disputes between the two houses was the "conference committee," in which both houses would appoint managers to meet to try to reach a compromise. With each house having equal votes, the process encouraged serious negotiations and was often successful.

By the 1850s, the original structure of the Province of Canada's upper house had been greatly altered. Its power with respect to money bills had been significantly reduced pursuant to section 57 of the *Union Act*, which stipulated "all Bills for appropriating any Part of the Surplus of the said Consolidated Revenue Fund, or for imposing any new Tax or Impost, shall originate in the Legislative Assembly." Residency requirements for members of the upper house had been proposed in 1846, and property qualifications for Legislative Councillors were made mandatory in 1856.

As previously noted, the Legislative Council had been made elective. Although this method of selection was done away with within ten years, the territorial arrangement agreed upon for distributing seats met with few objections. "Regional balance" was established in the upper house with equal representation from Canada West (Ontario) and from Canada East (Quebec). Once the appointed members who had been "grandfathered" vacated their seats, each section of the province would have an equal number of seats, with twenty-four members from Ontario and twenty-four from Quebec. The bones of the Senate of Canada can be traced directly to many of the features of the pre-Confederation upper chambers.

A fourth precept was that the Fathers were not bound to parliamentary institutions moulded along British lines. They understood the importance of Lord Durham's advice, who warned that trying to replicate the House of Lords would not work. Durham had stated: "The constitution of the House of Lords is consonant with the frame of English society; and ... the creation of a precisely similar body in such a state of society as that of these Colonies is impossible."[21]

In one of the first formal resolutions adopted at Quebec, it was agreed:

[t]hat in framing a Constitution for the General Government, the
Conference, with a view to the perpetuation of our connection with

the Mother Country, and to the promotion of the best interests of the people of these late Provinces, desire to follow the model of the British Constitution, as far as our circumstances will permit.[22]

Edward Whelan thought the point of the resolution lay in the words "as far as possible," meaning that the conference would "not be trammeled by too close an adherence to the forms of the British constitution."[23]

The Framework of the Senate

During the discussions in London, formal agreement on the Senate's structure and roles was reached. It took its legislative form in specific sections of the *Constitution Act, 1867*, most notably 17, 18, 21–26, 39, 53, and 91. The Senate's original framework can be summarized as follows.[24]

Distribution of Seats

The delegates attending the Quebec City conference focused first not on the Senate's powers or how senators were selected but with the chamber's territorial makeup. This was the most difficult issue. The Maritime provinces believed that "the only safeguard the smaller Provinces would possess was the Council" and bargained for more seats. Prince Edward Island pressed for equal representation.[25] Given the French–English imbalance in British North America, the Quebec delegates were steadfastly opposed to awarding each Maritime colony the same number of seats as Quebec. The Ontario delegates did not want the Senate to block the political influence it expected to have, given its population numbers.[26]

The agreement called for the equality of seats for each region, not province. On 17 October 1864, a motion was adopted that the upper house would be based on three divisions: "1st Upper Canada (Ontario); 2nd Lower Canada (Quebec); 3rd Nova Scotia, New Brunswick, and Prince Edward Island, with equal representation in the Legislative Council." Ontario was to have twenty-four members, Quebec twenty-four members, Nova Scotia ten, New Brunswick ten, and Prince Edward Island four.[27]

Adding a territorial component for the upper house was a defining departure from the House of Lords, rendering any future comparisons between the Senate and the House of Lords misleading. Also included was the provision that members from Quebec should represent electoral districts. Mackay writes: "Its purpose was to assure to both the French-speaking Roman Catholic majority and the English-speaking Protestant minority their fair share of representation in the upper house."[28]

The Federal Function

The Fathers saw the upper house as having an important regional role. Sir Étienne-Paschal Taché, the Premier of the Province of Canada, stated each region was given equal members "so as to secure to each province its rights, its privileges, and its liberties."[29] Alexander Galt, Canada's minister of finance, declared: "To the Legislative Council all the Provinces look for protection under the Federal principle."[30] Its regional function was emphasized in the marginal heading to section 22 of the *Constitution Act, 1867*, which read "Representation of Provinces in the Senate."

John A Macdonald stated: "To the Upper House is to be confided the protection of sectional interests; therefor is it that the three great divisions are there equally represented, for the purpose of defending such interests against the combinations of majorities in the Assembly." He felt the Senate's design went far beyond that of the House of Lords and compared the new Canadian upper house to the American Senate:

> It will, therefore, become the interest of each section to be represented by its very best men, and the members of the Administration who belong to each section will see that such men are chosen, in case of a vacancy in their section. For the same reason each

state of the American union sends its two best men to represent its interests in the Senate.[31]

Appointment of First Senators

Resolution Fourteen of the Seventy-Two Resolutions stated the first selection of members to the upper house would be made "from the Legislative Councils of the various Provinces … so that all political parties may, as nearly as possible, be fairly represented."[32] Having a diverse membership from all three regions would assist the upper chamber in carrying out its federal duties. Taché justified the restraint put on the power of the Crown to make appointments:

> [W]here there is partisanship there can be no justice. Where there is partisanship there can be no stability … It is only when justice is rendered to all parties that you can reckon upon stable and permanent governmental institutions. To shew the difference between the spirit which actuated these nominations, from 1841 to 1847, and the spirit which exists now, it is only necessary to refer to the resolutions of the Conference. The fourteenth resolution … shews you the spirit in which these resolutions were framed.[33]

Vincent Pouliot has commented:

> It is clear that the Fathers of Confederation intended that the provincial parties be fairly represented in the Senate. What is not clear is whether they meant to establish this as the principle underlying the representative character of the Senate, whether it was meant to guarantee only the representative character of the first Senate or whether it was to guarantee the representative character of the Senate until each province chose how it wished to be represented … If all provincial parties were proportionally represented in the Senate, then the provincial interests of the people, the people in their provincial political capacity or, put more simply, the provinces, would be truly represented in Parliament.[34]

As it turned out, as vacancies occurred, the traditional manner of appointments to the upper house was reinstated. No further restrictions were placed on the power of the federal government to summon qualified persons. Taché's plea to render justice "to all parties" when making appointments was forgotten.

Powers

The Fathers showed great reluctance in doing away with the older model of mixed government since they believed it still held value. Despite the acceptance of the responsible government, the co-equal legislative power arrangement enacted in 1791 for central Canada was repeated. In what became section 91 of the *Constitution Act, 1867*, the Senate was given identical power with the House of Commons regarding the adoption of laws. The section reads: "It shall be lawful for the Queen, by and with the Advice and Consent of the Senate and House of Commons, to make Laws for the Peace, Order and good Government of Canada."

John A Macdonald declared:

> There would be no use of an upper house if it did not exercise, when it thought proper, the right of opposing or amending or postponing the legislation of the lower house. It would be of no value whatever were it a mere chamber for registering the decrees of the lower house.[35]

AG Archibald of Nova Scotia agreed: "The Upper House may disagree with the House of Commons. Its value will be that of occasional obstruction." Hector-Louis Langevin, Canada's Postmaster General, agreed: "If you give power to swamp the Legislative Council then you destroy its utility."[36]

Resolving Intracameral Disputes

As noted above, the traditional method of resolving disagreements between the two houses had been to use conference committees. At the London Conference, despite Imperial efforts, the Canadian delegation resisted attempts to change this practice by implementing a more effective deadlock-breaking mechanism. Altering the provisions of the Quebec resolutions, which had purposely omitted a safety-valve, would threaten the whole agreement. Nova Scotia's Jonathan McCully said this kind of discussion was "now touching the very life of the whole scheme. If we err, the whole scheme will come down some time."[37]

Lord Carnarvon, Imperial Secretary of State for the Colonies, eventually succeeded in getting the Fathers to accept a weak swamping mechanism in the form of sections 26, 27, and 28, which provided for the appointment of up to six additional senators equally divided among the regional divisions. However, as Carnarvon told the British House of Commons: "I am free to confess that I could have wished that the margin had been broader."[38] The mixed government's method for resolving intracameral disputes through conference committees was retained as the favoured procedure.

Method of Appointment and Qualifications of Senators

The decision to appoint senators for life was a matter of compromise. The Province of Canada had adopted the elective principle in 1856. When the Quebec Conference opened, John A Macdonald stated: "Some are in favour of the elective principle. More are in favour of appointment by the Crown. I will keep my own mind open upon that point as if it were a new question to me altogether."[39] Taché later admitted:

> Some of us might have preferred still to retain the elective principle, but then we had to meet those gentlemen from below, and we had to give and take. We could not carry everything our own way. The gentlemen from the Lower Provinces were opposed to the elective principle, and went strongly for the system of appointments by the Crown.[40]

Life appointments gave the Senate a degree of independence from the House of Commons and from special interests. Macdonald believed: "It must be an independent House, having a free action of its own."[41] Brown had similar views: "The desire was to render the Upper House a thoroughly independent body — one that would be in the best position to canvass dispassionately the measures of this House, and stand up for the public interests in opposition to hasty or partisan legislation."[42] However, not all concurred with Macdonald's or Brown's assessment that the Senate would act independently. John S Sanborn, an elected Legislative Councillor, observed:

> If, in the very first instance, the prerogative is exercised, not by the Sovereign or the Sovereign's representative, unbiassed, but is exercised by a party government, you have a House constituted at its very first meeting of a party character.[43]

As for the qualification of senators, the Fathers agreed:

> [t]hat the members of the Legislative Council shall be British subjects, by birth or naturalization, of the full age of thirty years, shall possess a real property qualification of four thousand dollars over and above all incumbrances, and be worth that amount over and above their debts and liabilities.[44]

The conditions for disqualifying a senator were outlined in section 31: failure to attend two consecutive sessions; making an oath of allegiance to a foreign power; bankruptcy and insolvency; being convicted of treason or any "infamous crime"; and ceasing to be qualified in respect of residency. Many provisions were similar with those described in the *Union Act* of 1840 and *An Act to change the Constitution of the Legislative Council by rendering the same Elective*, adopted in 1856.

The Senate's Complementary Role

While lauding the virtues of mixed government, the Fathers understood that, with the rise of democracy, political power must be transferred to the House of Commons. Another model of bicameral theory — the complementary one in which an upper chamber's role would be non-threatening — had to be crafted into the Senate's architecture.

In the *Confederation Debates*, John A Macdonald pointed to the example of the House of Lords as a second chamber whose members do not challenge the lower house on essential matters:

> [E]ven the House of Lords … whenever it ascertains what is the calm, deliberative will of the people of England, it yields, and never in modern times has there been, in fact or act, any attempt to over-rule the decisions of (the Lower House) by the appointment of new peers.

Macdonald saw the Senate having "the sober second thought in legislation," which would "never set itself in opposition against the deliberative and understood wishes of the people." He added:

> And is it, then, to be supposed that the members of the upper branch of the legislature will set themselves deliberately at work to oppose what they know to be the settled opinions and wishes of the people of the country? They will not do it. There is no fear of a deadlock between the two houses.[45]

Conclusion

In designing the Senate, the Fathers borrowed from three theoretical models of bicameral institutions. They saw each contributing to an institutional architecture that best fitted with Canadian history, traditions, and political culture. By blending the models, none remained "pure" but were compromised in theory and design to accommodate the others. A pan-Canadian typology emerged to serve uniquely Canadian needs. The Senate's essential "nature," a linked hybrid constitutional and political model with three competing principles and roles — mixed government, territorial, and complementary — took form without precise definition as to model boundaries and no specification as to which was primary.

CHAPTER FOUR

The Roles of the Senate in Historical Perspective

In Chapter 3, we saw the Founding Fathers purposely designing the Senate as a hybrid institution consisting of three components: mixed government, whereby the two houses have equal legislative power; territorial, which focuses on representation and territorial protection; and complementary, in which the upper house uses influence to affect legislative change as opposed to confrontational political power.

The Fathers believed their "made-in-Canada" compromise was workable. Although the models had different purposes, they were linked. Through the discretionary and cautious exercise of constitutional power, legislative trade-offs could be bargained for to ensure the Senate's contribution to public policy would be positive for the nation and for the regions.

This chapter will trace how these three models have played out over the course of the Senate's history. Given that the Fathers first agreed on a territorial component, we will begin with examining this characteristic of the Senate's design and its impact on Canadian federalism.

Federalism

As noted, the Fathers expected the Senate to play an important role in Canadian federalism by providing greater regional representation in the policies of the national government. The verdict of most commentators is, however, that the Senate has had little impact. Gordon Robertson, a former clerk of the Privy Council, concluded the Senate "has failed to establish itself as the effective voice of regional interests that the Fathers of Confederation talked about and that the underlying conditions of federalism require." Michael Pitfield, also a former Privy Council clerk, concluded that in its "important role of regional representation, I believe the Senate has done a very poor job. This is a tragic failure because, particularly in a federation, this is a special, and in a sense, unique role for a second chamber." Professor Paul Thomas has observed: "The failure of the Senate to articulate and to mediate regional interests is widely regarded as its greatest failing."[1]

Dissatisfaction with the Senate's regional role began early. It took only seven years before a motion was made in the House of Commons by David Mills (subsequently a minister of justice):

> That the present mode of constituting the Senate is inconsistent with the Federal principle in our system of government, makes the Senate alike independent of the people, and of the Crown ... and our Constitution ought to be so amended as to confer upon each Province the power of selecting its own Senators, and to defining the mode of their election.[2]

There is much evidence supporting the conclusion the Senate has been ineffective. FA Kunz notes that while the Senate did defeat the Old Age Pensions bill in 1926 on the grounds it violated provincial jurisdiction over property and civil rights, it did not throw out the government's social welfare program in 1935, although the same reasoning could have been used. During the post-war period, the Senate neglected to protect the provinces in a host of bills, such as those dealing with family allowances, the Canadian Wheat Board, and the dairy industry.[3] In the 1980s, the Senate failed to overturn policies seen as discriminatory to Western provinces, for example, the National Energy Policy and the awarding of an aircraft-servicing contract to a Montreal firm, although a bid by a Winnipeg company was better and cheaper.[4]

The Senate's weakness can be traced to many sources. Some point to the incompatibility of the territorial model with parliamentary government. Kunz feels the Senate could never be destined to play the role of "the main and principal institutional protector of the federal units" since such a chamber "is incompatible with the fundamental principles of the British cabinet system, upon which the political regime of Canada was constructed."[5] Mackay notes: "parliamentary government required responsibility to the elected representatives of the people, and to none other."[6]

Others point to the increasing importance of the Cabinet. David E Smith writes: "There is no doubt that one of the features of Canadian federalism, the federalized cabinet, has lessened the importance of the Senate as an institution of regional opinion."[7] The judicial process and the use of federal–provincial conferences as ways to manage disputes have also impinged upon the Senate's regional role.

Others cite the constitutional limitation of selecting senators through appointment by the federal government, thus freeing them from local or electoral pressures. This point was argued by Christopher Dunkin, a member of the Legislative Assembly from Quebec, during the *Confederation Debates*. Dunkin believed that section 24 of the *Constitution Act, 1867* was fatal to making the Senate a protector of provincial interests. After the first group of senators retire and vacancies occur, he said:

> [T]hey are to be filled as we are now told — and this is the strangest thing of all — not by the provincial legislatures, nor by any authority or under any avowed influence of the local kind, but possibly by the General Government. And forsooth, this is called the Federal feature of our system![8]

Michael Pitfield made a similar point in 1984: "as an appointed chamber it simply does not carry the credibility necessary to perform the role (of regional representation) in this day and age."[9]

The fact that Western Canada is underrepresented in the Senate has also been cited. In 1915 the *Constitution Act, 1867* was amended to create a fourth division of Western provinces with twenty-four seats. That number has remained constant ever since, despite the West's growth in population and economically. Today, British Columbia and Alberta hold only 11.4 percent of Senate seats yet represent over 25 percent of Canada's population. Many feel that by increasing Western representation the Senate could play a more vital role in reflecting the federal character of Canada.

Donald Savoie sees a more profound reason. In a recent book, he concludes that most Canadian political institutions were built to serve the centre of the country. The "Ottawa system," based on representation by population, a Cabinet with strong representation from Ontario, and senior public servants concentrated in Ottawa, is structured to serve the "national interest." He writes:

> Canada's Fathers of Confederation set out to build institutions to fix the problems plaguing the old Canadas — now Ontario and Quebec. They have not been, and are still not, designed to accommodate the outer Canadas.[10]

In the confines of such a system of power, the Senate has limited opportunity to provide a regionally based check and balance on the popularly elected House of Commons.

Clearly, the dominance of party has been another factor. Historically, most of the appointments have reflected the partisanship of the party in power.[11] Canada's upper house is not alone among second chambers in which party concerns have vitiated against the discharge of constitutional functions. Jeremy Waldron observes that where there is party politics, "parties would naturally do what they could to ensure that their members in the second chamber were brought under the same discipline as their members in the first. There is probably no way of ruling that out."[12] Party politics has the potential of overriding the theoretical functions of second chambers. Vernon Bogdanor feels "the dominance of party politics in modern democracies" means that "the practice of bicameralism bears very little relation to the theory."[13]

Up until the changes in the appointment process brought in by Prime Minister Justin Trudeau in 2015, the Senate had been organized largely on party lines. Strategies on bills, seating plans, membership in committees, speaking lists in the chamber, the allocation of offices, and committee travel were often decided according to party, not region. There were few organized structures to allow senators to pursue regional objectives within the legislative process.

Despite their collective shortcomings in mitigating regional problems, many senators have used their positions to try to protect local interests. One successful attempt was the Maritime Code amendments of 1977. Bill C-14, introduced by the minister of transport and adopted by the House of Commons, would have done away with the local system of port shipping regulations and substituted instead one central registry for ships located in Ottawa. If the bill had passed, henceforth all registered ships in Canada would have displayed the name "Ottawa" at their stern. The Senate Transport and Communications Committee did not find the reasons to make this change persuasive and voted unanimously to return to the previous system whereby the actual registry of ships would be carried out in local ports. This change was accepted by the minster and the House of Commons.[14]

Senator Charles McElman (New Brunswick), who played a leading role in convincing the minster of transport to drop his proposal, spoke about the individual role of senators as regional representatives upon his retirement in 1990:

> [A]ppointment to the Senate does enable one to make an unique contribution in public affairs and the development of the nation, and more particularly, on behalf of the citizens of one's province and region. I do not hesitate for a moment to state that on a godly number of occasions, through representations made in regional

and national caucus and through direct representations to ministers of the Crown, I have been able to affect changes in policies and legislation to more properly reflect the interests and sensitivities of my own province, the region and our people. In some instances, I have been able to prevent actual injury to those interests that gives me much satisfaction ... I firmly believe it to be true that most members of this chamber can make that same statement with factual assurance. It is unfortunate that most Canadians are unaware of these facts.[15]

Parliamentary Government

Professor Ajzenstat writes: "The Second Chamber as the Canadian founders intended it had the vital function of checking the potential for highhandedness in Cabinet and Commons."[16] This function is less ambiguous than its regional role. Pursuant to section 91, the Senate's legislative powers are co-equal to those of the lower house. No bill can become law without the Senate's consent. It has the unrestricted constitutional right to defeat, delay, or amend any bill coming from the lower house.

Although there have been attempts to remove the Senate's veto and replace it with a suspensory one like that of the House of Lords, no such action has been successful.[17] Stripping the Senate of the power of veto, former Senator Serge Joyal believes, would reduce the Senate to nothing more than an advisory chamber. "The corollary of this would be, in theory, an all-powerful House of Commons, but, in practice, an omnipotent executive government."[18]

Section 91 links the territorial, mixed government, and complementary designs of the Senate. David E Smith writes:

> To accept only a suspensory veto would compromise (the Senate's) ability to play the roles it has created for itself, that is, to review, delay, negotiate, amend and defeat (if necessary) legislation it deems prejudicial to the interests it was created to protect. A suspensory veto would undermine a central part of the Canadian

federal scheme, because it would submit sectional interests, of which language and culture are quintessential Canadian examples, to majoritarian rule alone.[19]

The parliamentary record shows the Senate, while not abusing its veto power, has not backed away from defeating legislation sent to it from the House of Commons. The Senate Law Clerk and Parliamentary Counsel calculated that during the twentieth century, the Senate had used its veto power to defeat bills forty-four times.[20]

Political scientists have tried to find patterns in the Senate actions. Mackay notes that prior to 1925, the Senate was "frequently charged with being on the side of the vested interests rather than the public" as it played a pro-active role in protecting property rights of vested interests.[21] Kunz concluded that the Senate has a tradition of using its legislative powers to fight for the supremacy of Parliament against an ever-encroaching executive and to safeguard the rights of the individual. This was particularly evident in the Senate's defiance of the Diefenbaker government in 1961 regarding the removal of James E Coyne as governor of the Bank of Canada. When Mr Coyne refused to tender his resignation, as he was requested to do by the minister of finance, the government introduced Bill C-114, declaring his position vacant. Following its passage by the House of Commons, the Senate sent the bill to a committee where Mr Coyne, assisted by his officials, appeared as the sole witness. After a hearing that lasted seven sittings and over thirteen hours, the committee reported that Bill C-114 should not proceed any further. Mr Coyne then resigned. Kunz writes that in this and other cases "the Senate has acted in the capacity of a sort of institutional Ombudsman in the Canadian parliamentary system."[22]

Other examples of its checking function may be cited. In 1875, the Senate rejected a bill for the construction of a railway from Esquimalt to Nanaimo in British Columbia. In 1913 it defeated the Naval Assistance Bill, and in 1926, the Old Age Pensions Bill.[23] In the 1980s and early 1990s, when Senator Allan J MacEachen was leader of the Opposition and his party enjoyed an overwhelming majority in the upper chamber, the Senate regularly defied the House of Commons. Franks writes that MacEachen's appointment "began a series of confrontations between the two Houses the like of which had never been seen before." When it refused to pass legislation for a free trade deal with the United States in 1988, Franks observed: "The Senate achieved its greatest importance in history."[24]

Upon his retirement, Senator MacEachen referred to the Senate as a "sleeping giant" that had decided "to flex its legislative muscles." The source of the Senate's activism, he felt, was hardly illegitimate. "In the Senate, of course, we do have a source of authority. It is not as easily explained because our authority comes from the fundamental law of the land — the Constitution. The powers we have come from that Constitution."

But the Senate's powers needed to be used cautiously. MacEachen admitted:

> I am not arguing the rightness or wrongness of the actions taken by the Senate … It goes without saying that the Senate should survey the ground carefully and deliberate prudently, as I have heard it said, in exercising its legislative powers … [A]s a senator, I have had no electors. I was not mandated by a body of electors to represent them in Parliament … We also recognize the absence of the direct link of accountability with electors created through an election affects one's authority to speak in Parliament, in caucus and elsewhere.[25]

The historical record shows that senators have used their formidable powers with voluntary self-restraint. Andrew Heard believes there appears to be a general principle of how the Senate should deal with amendments to House of Commons bills:

> [I]t should not act to frustrate the general thrust of Commons legislation put before it … This rule would be based on the principle of the pre-eminence to be given to the elected Lower House by an appointed Upper House in a modern democracy.[26]

Review of Legislation

Of all its roles, the Senate's complementary function as "a chamber of sober second thought" is clearly its most accomplished. Savoie observes that senators do "what they know best, reviewing legislation."[27] Writing in 1965, Kunz concluded:

> It seems fair to say that the services rendered by the Senate … in form of technical amendments to government legislation have demonstrated its constructive capacity as a revisory body of great usefulness. The Senate has made a wide variety of important, though unspectacular, improvements in public bills, either on its own initiative or upon requests from the Government of the day.[28]

Its success as a complementary model can be attributed to several factors. Since it is not a confidence chamber, the Senate can focus its attention on public policy. The institutional features of the Senate are also beneficial. Senators function at a less pressured pace than members of the Commons and have greater procedural freedom and opportunities to raise legislative concerns. Professor Thomas writes: "A great deal of the Senate's time is, in fact, spent talking about legislation, matters that could lead to legislation, or concerns that arise out of experience with past legislation."[29]

As well, the Senate has a robust system of committees that perform at a high parliamentary standard. Many senators make committee work their priority. Constitutional scholar and former senator Eugene Forsey described the Senate's committee activities as follows:

> The Senate's main work is done in its committees, where it goes over bills clause by clause and hears evidence, often voluminous, from groups and individuals who would be affected by the particular bill under review. This committee work is especially effective because the Senate has many members with specialized knowledge and long years of legal, business or administrative experience.[30]

In Chapter 6, we shall examine case studies of the Senate at work, demonstrating the challenges and limitations senators face as they carry out their constitutional functions. The next chapter, however, will describe how the Senate is structured and its main institutional features.

CHAPTER FIVE

The Structure of the Senate

So far, we have focused on what the Senate is and what the Senate does. We will now examine how it carries out its work. This chapter will cover (1) the provisions regarding geographical representation; (2) the rules relating to membership and remuneration; (3) how proceedings in the chamber are conducted; (4) the work of its committees; and (5) the basic elements of the Senate's parliamentary procedure.

Geographical Representation

Originally, the Senate was composed of seventy-two members with twenty-four members from three divisions — Ontario, Quebec, and the Maritimes. The original agreement stated that Nova Scotia would have ten senators, New Brunswick ten, and Prince Edward Island four. When PEI refused to join the new federation, the twenty-four Maritime members were divided equally between New Brunswick and Nova Scotia. When Prince Edward Island entered Confederation in 1873, it did so on the original terms and conditions. In accordance with the *Constitution Act, 1867*, Senate representation of the Maritime provinces was to be readjusted as vacancies occurred.[1]

Resolution Ten of the Seventy-Two Resolutions stated: "The North-West Territory, British Columbia and Vancouver shall be admitted into the Union on such terms and conditions as the Parliament of the Federated Provinces shall deem equitable." The *Manitoba Act* gave the new province two senators, and as it grew, three, and then four. The *British Columbia Terms of Union* stipulated it would have three senators. The *Alberta Act* and the *Saskatchewan Act* provided for four senators each with the proviso "that such representation may … be from time to time increased to six by the Parliament of Canada." Pursuant to the *Constitution Act, 1915*, Western Canada was recognized as a separate division and allotted a representation of 24 members.[2]

The Fathers regarded Newfoundland as a distinct region. John A Macdonald felt the province had sectional interests and claims of its own: "It, therefore has been treated separately, and is to have a separate representation in the Upper House, thus varying from the equality established between the other sections."[3] The province entered Confederation only in 1949 with a representation of six senators.[4]

Pursuant to the *Constitution Act, 1975*, the Northwest Territories and the Yukon Territory were allotted one senator each. They were not added to an existing region but, like Newfoundland and Labrador, treated as exceptions to sectional divisions. The Territory of Nunavut, created in accordance with the *Nunavut Act* of 1993, is represented in the Senate by one member.[5]

Today, the total number of senators is 105, and the provincial and territorial representation of senators is as follows:

- Ontario: 24
- Quebec: 24
- Nova Scotia: 10
- New Brunswick: 10
- Prince Edward Island: 4
- Newfoundland and Labrador: 6
- Manitoba: 6
- Saskatchewan: 6
- Alberta: 6

- British Columbia: 6
- Yukon: 1
- Northwest Territories: 2
- Nunavut: 1

Section 23 of the *Constitution Act, 1867* requires that senators own land worth at least $4,000 in the province for which they are appointed and be a resident there. In the case of Quebec, a senator must have their real property qualification in the electoral division for which they are appointed or be a resident in that division.

Administratively, the Senate recognizes that travel is a necessary component of the geographical representation of senators and has established policies to pay for travel to and from primary residences to attend sittings and committee meetings. Such policies also recognize that the parliamentary functions of senators require them to travel within their regions.

All senators have access to the same travel resources regardless of which province or territory they live. As well, senators may rent commercial space for a regional office.[6]

Membership and Remuneration

Senators must be at least thirty years old, a natural-born subject of the Queen, and own property worth at least $4,000 above all debts. Senators can be disqualified for various reasons, such as failing to attend two consecutive sessions of Parliament, being convicted of a felony, or ceasing to be qualified in respect or property or residence.

Originally senators could hold their place for life, but on 1 June 1965, the provision was amended so that senators serve only until they are seventy-five years old.[7] When a vacancy occurs by resignation or death, the Governor General is authorized to summon "a fit and qualified" person. There is no timeline for doing so.[8]

In 2008, the Senate adopted a conflict-of-interest code, now renamed the *Ethics and Conflict of Interest Code for Senators*. The Code contains provisions that aim to ensure that senators serve the public interest and those they represent to the best of their abilities. In 2014 the Code was amended to state that senators perform their parliamentary duties with "dignity, honour and integrity." A senator is forbidden to act or attempt in any way to further their own private interests when performing parliamentary functions or improperly further any other person's private interests. The Code is administered by the Senate ethics officer, an independent officer of the Senate. Pursuant to section 33 of the *Constitution Act, 1867*, questions relating to the qualification of a senator or a vacancy in the Senate are determined by the Senate itself.[9]

For fiscal year 1 April 2021, senators were paid a sessional indemnity of $160,800. By comparison, the basic sessional indemnity of members of the House of Commons is $185,800.[10] Senators outside the Parliamentary District have access to a living expenses budget.

Proceedings in the Senate Chamber

Within Commonwealth parliaments, the position of Speaker has been described as "the linchpin of the whole chariot."[11] The Speaker presides over the proceedings of the chamber and regulates debate, maintains decorum, and decides points of order, subject to appeal to the Senate. They may vote on all questions and must vote at the same time as other senators. Unlike their counterpart in the House of Commons, the Senate Speaker cannot break a tie.

The proceedings are recorded in its daily records, specifically the *Journals of the Senate*, the *Order Paper and Notice Paper*, and the *Debates of the Senate*. The *Journals* are the permanent record of the chamber and state chronologically what has taken place that sitting day, for example the petitions presented, the reading of bills, matters referred to committees, votes taken, and which debates are adjourned. The *Journals* are based on the Clerk's Scroll, which is handwritten in the Senate chamber by the clerk of the Senate, assisted by the other table officers. It includes lists of senators who were present or who were in attendance to business pursuant to the *Senators Attendance Policy*. The rulings and statements by the Speaker are also recorded.

The *Order Paper and Notice Paper* is the Senate's official agenda and carries the items that may be called during the day's sitting. The *Order Paper* also publishes, on a weekly basis, the list of unanswered written questions from senators that seek statistical or other information.

The *Debates of the Senate*, also referred to as *Hansard*, is the record of speeches made in the Senate. The debates are reported verbatim, although minor corrections may be made. Senate proceedings are also recorded through video broadcasting, accessible through the parliamentary network and on the Senate's own website.

Calling the government to account is done through four specific procedures: Question Period, Written Questions, Motions, and Inquiries. The daily thirty-minute Question Period allows senators to pose questions to the Leader of the Government in the Senate or to their representative regarding any aspect of government policy. Government ministers who sit in the House of Commons are sometimes invited to attend the Senate Question Period and answer questions. Written questions are used to inquire on the more technical points of government policy. Motions are substantial in nature, in which senators express a stated position or call for further public action. Inquiries, which are not voted upon, allow senators to call the attention of the Senate to matters of public policy.

A large part of the proceedings is taken up with debate. A wide variety of subjects are discussed. Recent examples include the presence of racism and discrimination within Canadian institutions, the weaknesses in Canada's long-term care system, immigration, and issues relating to international affairs. Such debates generate publicity for the subject at hand and may influence future agenda-setting by the government.

In terms of legislation, a bill goes through the same stages as in the House of Commons, although there are certain differences in the procedures followed. Most bills adopted by the Senate have originated in the House of Commons and are government bills.[12]

Stage One is first reading, in which the bill is presented by the sponsoring senator and the title read out by a table officer. Since senators have the right to present a bill, no advance notice is required.

Stage Two is second reading, in which the bill is debated. This stage focuses on the principle of the bill. When the debate closes, the Speaker will put the question. If the motion to read the bill a second time is adopted, a table officer will say: "Second reading of this bill." Although a bill may proceed directly to a third reading, bills are usually referred to a committee for further consideration. The motion for committee referral is not debatable.

Stage Three is committee stage, in which each clause of the bill is considered. Amendments may be proposed.

Stage Four is report stage, in which the bill is reported back to the chamber by the chair of the committee that examined it. If the bill is reported without amendment, the report will be deemed adopted and the senator sponsoring the bill will move it be read a third time at the next sitting. If the committee reports the bill with amendments, it will be debated and voted upon. A committee cannot make any change without the concurrence of the Senate. If amendments are adopted, a motion will be made for the bill's third reading as amended, usually at the next sitting of the Senate.

Stage Five is third reading. Amendments may again be proposed. When the motion for third reading has been adopted and the bill passed, the Speaker will direct that a message be sent to the House of Commons informing that House of the Senate's decision. If there is disagreement between the two chambers, further amendments may be proposed with the bill going back and forth as in a game of "Ping-Pong." A bill must be passed in identical form by both Houses before it can become law.

Stage Six, the final stage, is royal assent, which is the signification of the Crown's acceptance of the bill. It is granted by the Governor General or by one of the Governor General's deputies, such as a justice of the Supreme Court. Pursuant to the *Royal Assent Act*, assent must be signified in the Senate chamber in the presence of the three constituent entities of Parliament (the Queen or her representative, the Senate, and the House of Commons) at least twice a year. Most often it is signified by written declaration at a ceremony at Rideau Hall.

At times, the Senate examines the subject matter of a bill while it is still before the House of Commons. A pre-study allows senators to report their preliminary conclusions before they have formally received the bill, allowing the lower house an opportunity to take the views of senators into consideration before completing its own proceedings. Even if pre-studies have been conducted, the Senate follows due process, requiring bills to pass through three readings before they are adopted.

Committee Work

Senate committees traditionally have been seen as "the jewel of the Senate." Kunz writes:

> [A] considerable part of the Senate's functions is performed in committee and that in many cases what happens in the Chamber is only a preparation for, or a consummation of, what is accomplished in the committee room.[13]

The evolution of the Senate's committee system reflects in many ways the social, economic, and political history of Canada. In 1867, there were only three standing committees: Banking, Commerce, and Railways; Contingent Accounts; and Standing Orders and Private Bills. In 1879, the Banking, Commerce, and Railways Committee was divided into two: Banking and Commerce; and Railways, Telegraphs, and Harbours. In 1889, a standing committee on divorce was created.[14] In 1909, the following committees were added: Agriculture and Forestry; Immigration and Labour; Commerce and Trade Relations of Canada; and Public Health and Inspection of Food. In 1938, reflecting Canada's more independent constitutional status pursuant to the *Statute of Westminster 1931*, a committee on external relations was established, later renamed the Standing Committee on Foreign Affairs.

Presently, the Senate committee system includes the following: Agriculture and Forestry; Banking, Trade, and Commerce; Fisheries and Oceans; Energy, the Environment, and Natural Resources; Legal and Constitutional Affairs; National Finance; Aboriginal Peoples; Human Rights; National Security and Defence; Official Languages; Transport and Communications; and Social Affairs, Science, and Technology. Special committees and subcommittees may also be established. The Senate also participates with the House of Commons in joint committees, both standing and special.

Committees are noted for their policy investigations and cover a wide variety of subjects. Most recently, these have included reforming Indigenous education, financing the family farm, forestry issues, consumer protection in the financial service sector, digital currency, the lobster fishery, controlling foreign influence in Canadian elections, and modernizing the *Official Languages Act*.

There has never been a shortage of witnesses. Between 2015 and 2020, an average of 1,700 witnesses per year appeared before the committees of the Senate.[15] Paul Pross has observed that interest groups pay a great deal of attention to Parliament, particularly its committees, finding it useful to exploit their legitimizing and publicizing capacities.[16] Senate committee meetings are televised, and witnesses are given the opportunity to speak to senators and Canadians on public issues.

In addition to taking testimony in Ottawa, committees hold meetings and fact-finding missions outside the capital at local and regional levels, when so authorized.

Parliamentary Procedure in the Senate

A description of the Senate's procedural practices can be found in the numerous resources available on the Senate's website. However, given the many rules and unwritten parliamentary traditions, proceedings can sometimes appear overwhelming. A better understanding of Senate practice may be obtained by focusing on its fundamental principles. These may be summarized as follows: (1) the law of publicity; (2) the impartiality of the presiding officer; (3) the Senate's decision-making process; (4) freedom of speech; and (5) the majority principle.[17] Each of these will be described below.

The Law of Publicity

To make proper decisions, it is paramount senators never be taken by surprise. One of the Senate's most fundamental rules is that substantive proposals be given proper notice. The general notice requirement before any new proposal can be introduced is two sitting days. There are categories of motions that do not require notice,[18] but these do not involve "new" issues of substance. For example, no notice is required for a motion to adjourn the Senate or to adjourn the debate, since such motions can be moved at any time. Nor is notice required for an amendment to a motion. If an amendment goes too far and starts proposing ideas outside the scope of the original question, it is judged to be introducing "new" matter and should be ruled out of order. However, with the unanimous consent of all senators, the law of publicity may be waived.

The Absolute Impartiality of the Presiding Officer

The Speaker is both the judge and servant of the Senate and must not only be impartial but appear to be impartial. Confidence in the impartiality of the Speaker to act fairly and judiciously is an indispensable condition for the successful working of the Senate.

The Decision-Making Process

Senate decisions follow a process of three distinct and separate stages: (1) a motion, (2) a debate, and (3) a decision. First, a motion is formally made after due notice. Second, in accordance with its place on the order paper, and after it has been read to the chamber by the Speaker, debate begins. Although it may be interrupted pursuant to the Senate's adjournment rules, debate carries on until the last senator has had the opportunity to speak. Third, once the debate has concluded, the Senate will be ready for the question. A vote will take place to decide whether the motion is amended, passed, or defeated. Without the Senate's consent, the motion cannot be considered again in the same session. To move away from this sequence causes disorder and the inefficient use of the time of the chamber.

Several procedural rules flow from this basic process. Some examples are (1) when a matter is under debate, there can only be one question on the Senate floor at one time; (2) all debate must be relevant to the proposition before the chamber; remarks that are not relevant are out of order; (3) a senator can speak only once to a question; and (4) if an amendment is proposed, a new sequence begins since the amendment is regarded as a new question that supersedes debate on the original question. Even if a senator has spoken on the original question, once an amendment is proposed the senator may speak again since it is a new proposition. Debate on an amendment may also be superseded if an amendment to the amendment (a sub-amendment) is proposed.

Freedom of Speech

The right of free speech is the cornerstone of parliamentary privilege. The Mace, which precedes the Speaker in the parade at the opening of every sitting, symbolizes the right of senators to speak freely while in the chamber or in committee. This right is guaranteed in *The Bill of Rights 1689*, which declared that freedom of speech in Parliament "ought not to be impeached or questioned in any court or place outside of parliament." Without such freedom of speech, full and intelligent debate is jeopardized, and parliamentary privilege becomes a sham. The principle of free speech underscores the importance of privilege to the functioning of the Senate. All business no matter how crucial to the public interest will be set aside when meaningful questions of privilege are raised and found by the Speaker to have a *prima facie* basis.[19]

The Majority Principle

While the laws of parliamentary procedure embrace the concept of full and extensive debate on the issues of the day, they also recognize that at some point the will of the majority must have its way. Guillotine and time allocation motions, which require the Senate to decide a question by a particular date or at the end of a specified time, if not abused, are legitimate tools for the proper functioning of any legislative chamber.

In Chapter 6, we will look at examples of the Senate operating within its core models, and how it has performed, by analyzing four specific case studies.

CHAPTER SIX

The Senate at Work: Four Case Studies

This chapter will examine studies undertaken by senators within the context of the real-life workings of Parliament. As David E Smith has noted: "[T]he legitimacy of the Senate … rests in its activity."[1] The inquiries selected represent the various elements of the Senate's constitutional structure. They are examples of how senators carry out their work, and the challenges and limitations they encounter.

The first two — the 1987 study of Bill C-22, *An Act to amend the Patent Act and to provide for certain matters in relation thereto*, and the 1995 inquiry into the cancellation of the agreements regarding the redevelopment of Toronto's Pearson Airport — look at the Senate's legislative influence within the mixed government framework. The third surveys the 1968–71 Special Committee on Poverty and demonstrates its complementary role. The fourth study, the 1996 Special Committee on the Cape Breton Development Corporation, is selected as an example of the Senate's territorial function.

Bill C-22, *An Act to Amend the Patent Act*, 1987

In late 1986, the Progressive Conservative government of Brian Mulroney introduced Bill C-22, which gave patent holders of brand-name drugs ten years of freedom from competition. The government justified the bill on the grounds that spending on research would increase and be beneficial to Canada. Critics countered that Bill C-22 would cause drug prices to rise.[2] While the bill was supported by the Province of Quebec and the Pharmaceutical Association of Canada, it was opposed by various consumer groups, labour unions, church organizations, registered nurses, and senior citizens.

The political environment contributed greatly to the controversy over Bill C-22. Even though the governing Progressive Conservatives enjoyed a large majority in the House of Commons, the Opposition Liberal Party had the greatest number of seats in the Senate. Even before the proceedings on Bill C-22 began, the government had taken the position that it was not accountable to the Senate and would not acknowledge the Senate as a legitimate bargaining player.

In 1985, the Senate delayed a government borrowing bill and the following year made amendments to *An Act to amend the Parole Act and the Penitentiary Act* (the "gating" amendments), which resulted in Parliament being recalled from its summer recess. A period of intense partisanship between the two chambers had begun. Even though the Senate withdrew its *Parole Act* amendments, the leader of the Opposition in the Senate, Senator Allan J MacEachen, rejected the idea that the Senate must never interfere with the popular mandate given to the House of Commons. He noted the "modern Senate" had broken out of a pattern of refusing to participate more fully in its legislative role and that "it encourages me to believe that in the future the Senate can take on a more responsible legislative function."[3]

This change in the Senate's traditional workways did not go unnoticed by the supporters of the government. Senator Lowell Murray commented:

> The Honourable Senators we saw coming into the meeting of the National Finance Committee these past few weeks are not the Honourable Senators we have been accustomed to working with in that committee for the past four or five years. What we saw

coming into that committee was a hit team under the leadership of the Leader of the Opposition — a hit team inspired by frustration, bitterness and vengeance.[4]

Bill C-22 arrived in the Senate on 7 May 1987. Following second reading, it was referred not to a standing committee, which was the usual practice, but to a special committee that conducted cross-country meetings and heard from over 200 witnesses. The committee reported on 12 August with ten formal amendments. The Commons replied to these amendments on 2 September, saying it had agreed to part of one amendment but disagreed with most others as they contradicted the principle of the bill. The Commons did however propose two additional amendments. Its message was referred to the Banking, Trade, and Commerce Committee, which conducted further hearings and reported on 21 October, proposing additional amendments.

On 17 November, as in a game of "ping-pong," the Commons responded that it agreed to part of another amendment, disagreed with all others, and proposed two additional ones. These were concurred in by the Senate on 19 November. MacEachen said his party would accept the amendments and not defeat Bill C-22 because:

> the defeat of the bill today could become a victory for the government. Its energies could then be devoted to fanning the flames of regional grievances. It would blame the Senate for denying the people the alleged benefits of Bill C-22. In these circumstances, and in our system, it is much more appropriate that the government take the responsibility for the impact of the legislation rather than the Senate should do so.[5]

The Senate did manage concessions from the government in the final version of the bill in the following areas: (1) definitions; (2) calculating payments to the provinces; (3) proclaiming the bill into force; (4) making the English and French versions of some sections of the bill conform; (5) the powers of the Prices Review Board; (6) the information patentees must provide the board; and (7) the information to be contained in the board's annual report.

The legislative confrontation over Bill C-22 set the stage for other clashes over the next few years: Bills C-55 and C-84, both amending the *Immigration Act* (1988); Bill C-130, the *Canada-United States Free Trade Agreement Implementation Act* (1988); Bill C-103, the *Government Organization Act, Atlantic Canada, 1987* (1988); Bill C-21, *An Act to amend the Unemployment Insurance Act and the Employment and Immigration Department and Commission Act* (1989); and Bill C-62, dealing with the Goods and Services Tax (GST) (1990).[6] Although defeat of the government was never in question, legislative gridlock was uncharacteristically appearing in the Canadian Parliament. Bill C-22 showed the potential of the Senate responding in concrete political ways to government actions and becoming an important access point in the legislative process for disaffected groups, particularly around social policy.

Most senators did not see their power of amending legislation as restricted by the *Constitution Act, 1867*, nor their actions limited to "technical" amendments. However, the Liberal majority in the Senate knew they had to move cautiously, as their moral authority to substantially amend government legislation was clearly challenged. Its propensity to fight was limited. Given the appointed nature of the Senate, what changes the Senate made to Bill C-22 were basically administrative in nature and not matters involving the principles upon which the bill's policies were based.

The Pearson Airport Inquiry, 1995

In the general election held in 1993, the Liberal Party defeated the Progressive Conservatives and won an overwhelming majority in the House of Commons. However, in contrast to 1985, it was now the Progressive Conservatives who had the largest share of Senate seats. The new leader of the Opposition, Senator John Lynch-Staunton, claimed his colleagues would not do what the Liberals had done under Senator MacEachen — obstruct for the sake of obstruction. Lynch-Staunton later explained:

[T]his approach, attractive as it appeared, was abandoned in favour of one intended to return the Senate to what it was originally created to be: a chamber of sober second thought, respectful of decisions of the elected house, conscious of its responsibility to improve on them or, as the case may be, to warn of any legal and constitutional flaws to the point of defeating such bills if not corrected.[7]

The Special Committee on the Pearson Airport Agreements was established on 4 May 1995. It was launched in response to a government bill that sought to cancel contracts agreed to by the previous government for the redevelopment of Toronto's Pearson Airport. The Conservative majority in the Senate accused the new government of denying the right of those affected by the cancellation to seek damages in court. It wished to hold the government to account for why the contracts were cancelled.

At its organizational meeting of 8 June 1995, the committee signalled it would be an inquiry "pas commes les autres." In an unusual step for Senate committees, it structured itself along quasi-judicial lines by engaging the services of a legal counsel and empowering him to participate in the proceedings by asking questions of witnesses. As well, the committee agreed that all witnesses appearing would be required to take an oath or solemn affirmation to "tell the truth, the whole truth and nothing but the truth" and testify in public. The chair and deputy chair justified the procedure, saying it would "impress upon the witnesses ... the seriousness of the inquiry ... The committee was determined to get at the facts."[8]

Although its right to administer an oath was based on the *Parliament of Canada Act*,[9] the committee would not insist on answers. While it had the theoretical power to demand witnesses be forthcoming, the committee was aware it did not have the power of sanction. That power belonged only to the Senate, which was not planning to sit while the Pearson Airport Committee held its meetings. As well, the committee acknowledged the validity of the oaths that public servants and ministers took, by which they were not to disclose matters without due authority.

The committee's right to call for papers, records, and persons also faced obstacles. The government insisted that "disclosure of Cabinet records is regulated by the Privy Councillor's Oath and by the concept that Cabinet decisions are advice to the Sovereign which may only be revealed with his consent."[10]

Senate Counsel advised the committee to ask for all documents directly relative to the cancellation of the agreements. The justice department replied they would comply with the request but noted:

> Of these documents, some were Cabinet Confidences and therefore have been excluded … Certain others have been excluded because they are subject to solicitor-client privilege. Others have been excluded in whole or in part because they contain confidential business information.[11]

Many of the papers delivered to the committee contained "white-outs." The department officials who appeared recognized the extensive legal powers of the Senate to order the production of documents but said they had to be tempered with well-known practices and conventions.[12] The committee was never fully satisfied as to its access to government documents and its treatment by the government in this regard. The information was often not available in a timely fashion; there was inconsistent and excessive editing; too often there were claims of solicitor–client privilege; and there was a failure to obtain key Treasury Board documents as the interpretation of Cabinet confidences by the government seemed too broad.

While the setting within the Pearson Airport inquiry had the potential of terminating as a typical "opposition–government" standoff, in fact it did not. Despite the political wrangling, a *modus vivendi* was reached by which the government acknowledged that the Senate committee had a legitimate function to fulfill within the parliamentary process. While the government refused to hand over to the committee key documents, it was prepared to allow senators to ask questions of officials familiar with the issues about what was in the Treasury Board submissions upon which the decision to cancel the agreements was made. While the structures of Cabinet confidence were observed in theory, in practice the committee was satisfied it had obtained the information needed.

Following the presentation of the committee's report on 13 December 1995, the Senate turned its attention to Bill C-28, *An Act respecting certain agreements concerning the redevelopment and operation of Terminals 1 and 2 at Lester B. Pearson International Airport.* The government was unable to secure passage of the bill in the Senate before the session was prorogued. The bill never received royal assent.

The Special Committee on Poverty, 1968–1971

Poverty in Canada: A Report of the Special Senate Committee is regarded as a landmark study of the issue and remains one of the most influential reports the Senate has ever produced. It has been described as a "keystone for all later studies, parliamentary or otherwise."[13]

Its success may be attributed to many factors, including the dedication of its chair, Senator David Croll. A noted social reformer during the Depression when he was mayor of Windsor, Ontario, Croll served in the provincial Cabinet of Premier Mitch Hepburn and would later resign over whether the government was justified in sending in militia and provincial police to break up a strike of automobile workers. Croll said at the time, "My place is marching with the workers rather than riding with General Motors." After war service, he was elected to the House of Commons. In 1954 he was appointed to the Senate on the recommendation of Prime Minister Louis St Laurent, which some saw as an attempt to quiet him. Croll claimed: "I was not led, I was pushed," flatly declaring "I am not going to be an ornament." As a senator, he continued to advocate for the reform of social policies.[14]

Senator Croll attributed the success of the *Poverty Report* to the fact that it had come from the Senate, which was known and respected for its policy-oriented inquiries. His approach was markedly different from that taken later by Senators MacEachen and Lynch-Staunton. He did not seek confrontation with the House of Commons. He did not accuse the elected members of not doing their job. His tone was not overtly critical of the government of the day for not doing more to fight poverty. He and his colleagues were simply raising the issue. As Croll stated:

> But after three years of constant confrontation with poverty across Canada; of seeing first-hand the consequences of this sickness; after talking to the poor and poverty stricken and hundreds of lay and professional persons, the committee members emerged from this experience with a new outlook and a determination to bring about a new beginning and to begin a meaningful dialogue with the Canadian people. We don't pretend that the Report of Poverty is the best report that could have been written. Its impact lies in the fact that it came from the Senate. It's now on the Agenda. The dialogue has begun.[15]

The inquiry's origins lay in a recommendation made by the Economic Council of Canada, which suggested that a Senate committee involve itself in finding solutions to poverty. The council felt "the work of such a committee could do much to define and elucidate the problem of poverty in Canada, and to build public support for a more effective structure of remedial measures."

On 8 October 1968, Croll proposed a motion to establish a special committee to report "upon all aspects of poverty in Canada whether urban, rural, regional or otherwise, to define and elucidate the problem of poverty in Canada, and to recommend appropriate action." He believed senators were better qualified to undertake this study than a royal commission. They have "experience, know-how, capacity, and our committee could be composed of representatives from every province ... We are not a one-shot affair. We are a continuing body that can well follow up its recommendations."[16]

During its study, the committee travelled to all provinces as well as the Yukon, holding nearly 100 public hearings. It received over 200 briefs and heard from over 800 witnesses. The Library of Parliament has summarized the report's impact as follows:

The government realized the poor need more opportunity to have direct say in the policies affecting them … Responding to the need for regular expression of such views, the government reorganized the National Council on Welfare, an advisory body to the Minister of National Health and Welfare. Civil servants on the ground were replaced by strong representation of the poor … [T]he Committee's real importance manifested itself not so much in the government response to its recommendations, as in its role as a catalyst for organizing the poor in Canada and drawing attention to poverty.[17]

The committee made several recommendations, which included the implementation of a Guaranteed Annual Income and the creation of the Council of Applied Social Research. Some observers felt it could have gone further, especially in pressing the government to establish a Guaranteed Annual Income. During the study, tensions had built up between Croll and senior committee staff, who feared the chair was willing to compromise on recommendations as the government sought re-election. Some resigned. At the end of the inquiry, two reports were issued: the official committee report, *Poverty in Canada*, and a second document, *The Real Poverty Report*, written by Ian Adams and three other committee researchers and writers.[18]

It was unclear what those dissenting from the official report expected Croll to do. He was not in a leadership position. By his own account, the programs the committee proposed would cost around $900 million. Pursuant to section 53 of the *Constitution Act, 1867*, the Senate was prevented from appropriating any part of the public revenue on its own. The initiative for a Guaranteed Annual Income had to come from the Cabinet. As some have noted, there was little difference between the recommendations in the official committee report and the dissenting one. One commentator felt that what split Senator Croll and the dissenters was both personal and generational.[19]

The committee's report became a best-seller among government documents. The Library of Parliament noted the *Globe and Mail* called the report "Canada's first honest approach to poverty," while the *Montreal Star* suggested the real value of the report was not that it offered new insights on the issue but that it "legitimized insights already offered by others."[20]

The Special Committee on the Cape Breton Development Corporation, 1996

While there is a clear constitutional justification for the Senate's territorial role, the overwhelming consensus among observers is that the Senate has failed to establish itself as an effective voice of regional interests. As previously noted, it has been criticized for not developing a regionally based system of checks and balances on the House of Commons or becoming a key institution to give regional–provincial interests a powerful voice.

This is far from saying that the Senate has not played any regional role. Kunz provides numerous references to senators intervening on behalf of their local districts and championing such causes as agriculture, fishing, and shipping. He references a statement in 1950 by Senator Norman Platt Lambert:

> The provinces have a vital federal interest: it exists in the common ground of mutual relations in trade and commerce, in taxation, in defence, in social standards and security. In short, it exists in the sphere of all-around national welfare. Our duty is to see that matters of concern to the provinces are clearly and definitely presented here ... and that unity of democratic purpose shall be promoted throughout this land.[21]

Although the Senate was never a citadel of provincial rights, it has not ignored the role of asking the federal government to pay attention to specific regional anxieties. One example is the 1996 study of the Cape Breton Development Corporation.

The Cape Breton Development Company (Devco) was a federal Crown corporation established in 1967 to operate coal mines in Cape Breton, Nova Scotia, and to develop new economic opportunities in the surrounding communities. By 1996, the economic viability of the corporation was uncertain. In March of that year, Senator Lowell Murray, whose father had been a mine inspector for the province, raised the issue of having a special committee of the Senate examine the state of the Cape Breton Development Corporation and consider its future.

Senator Murray noted that Devco had recently announced the elimination of 400 permanent jobs with further layoffs over the next three years, adding to the unemployment rate for Cape Breton, which already stood at 20 percent. He told the Senate:

> The future of Devco is hanging in the balance today as management and the federal government, which is the sole shareholder, consider alternative courses of action ... There are the public statements of management, of federal government officials, and of cabinet ministers over the past several months ... All of these seem to be based on one overriding assumption, and that is that the only viable Cape Breton coal industry is a drastically reduced industry. Honourable senators, that assumption needs to be challenged. It needs to be critically examined. It needs to be defended and explained before a parliamentary committee, if only because the assumption is so much at variance with what we have been told by Devco under successive governments for at least 15 years.[22]

Senator MacEachen, whose own father had worked in the coal mines for over forty years, agreed but saw the inquiry as limited. He hoped the committee:

> can facilitate — not displace, but facilitate — a process that will result in a sound policy that will be acceptable and, in particular, that will ease the current and long-term anxieties that exist among the coal miners and within their communities and will give us all some hope that the Cape Breton coal industry will contribute to the future welfare of the people of Cape Breton.[23]

On 25 April 1996, the Senate created a special committee to examine the annual report and corporate plan of the Cape Breton

Development Corporation. The committee held public hearings in Sydney, Nova Scotia, and in Ottawa and issued three reports. While in Cape Breton, members visited some of the mines and witnessed firsthand underground operations and activities. The numerous witnesses, especially those representing labour unions, appreciated the Senate committee's visit and sympathetic ear, especially with respect to pension liability. In some ways, the hearings represented the old saying that everyone hates the Senate until they need them.

The chair, Senator William Rompkey, made it clear at the outset of the Sydney hearing that the committee did not set policy but could only make recommendations: "We are not decision-makers; however, we do have the power of recommendation; we have the power of public observation; and we have the power of people."

The committee's June 1996 report took an optimistic tone, giving Devco advice on what it saw as the best possible chance for commercial success and encouraging the participation of the federal government and the province of Nova Scotia in the future of Cape Breton's coal mining industry. It made proposals relating to corporate governance, marketing strategies, labour–management relations, and the future of mining operations. The committee claimed it was pleased with the reception given to its June report.

However, by the end of 1998, serious obstacles still stood in the way of Devco's commercial viability. Both of its mines had experienced shutdowns caused by geological and mechanical problems, and the operating shortages were in the millions of dollars. Devco ceased operation in 2009 and was amalgamated with Enterprise Cape Breton Corporation.

Conclusion

These four studies show the Senate independently carrying out functions in accordance with its underlying constitutional principles, namely those of mixed government, adding value to the political process through a complementary relationship with the House of Commons, and representation of territorial interests. The outcomes they produced varied, and also reflected the limitations of the Senate as an appointed chamber. Functioning as a model of mixed government, it was able to achieve administrative changes to Bill C-22, *An Act to amend the Patent Act,* but unable to stop the bill from proceeding through Parliament. It was successful, however, in preventing Bill C-28, dealing with the redevelopment of the Pearson Airport, from obtaining royal assent and becoming law. In its role as a complementary chamber, the report *Poverty in Canada* drew nationwide attention to the issue and helped build greater public support for the idea of a Guaranteed Annual Income. It was never the Senate's intention to exercise its broad constitutional powers to persuade the government to implement key committee recommendations. With respect to carrying out regional duties, the Special Committee on the Cape Breton Development Corporation provided a platform to highlight the problems facing the mining industry in Cape Breton and made helpful suggestions to improve Devco's commercial success. The Senate was unable, however, to generate sufficient political support in preventing further layoffs and the continued downsizing of the corporation's operations.

Next, in Chapter 7, we will examine the efforts made since 2015 to revive Canadian bicameralism by creating a Senate that functions with less partisan workways.

CHAPTER SEVEN

Reviving Canadian Bicameralism: The Non-partisan, Complementary Senate

On 29 January 2014, Justin Trudeau, then Liberal leader in the House of Commons, issued a statement saying that "the Senate is broken and needs to be fixed." Canada's second chamber, he claimed, was suffering from two central problems: partisanship and patronage. Outside of reopening the Constitution, which he felt Canadians did not want to do — "They don't want a long, rancorous, and likely pointless debate with the provinces that would distract us from focusing on more important problems" — his remedy for repairing the Senate was to make it a non-partisan, complementary institution. It would be composed of "thoughtful individuals representing the varied values, perspectives and identities of this great country" who were "independent from any particular political brand." He committed to changing the process that saw senators "appointed by one person, and one person only" and promised to put in place "an open, transparent, non-partisan public process for appointing and confirming Senators."

He also noted that "as an unelected body, there are — and ought to be — limits on the Senate's power. These limits have expanded over time and become conventions. These proposals are in keeping with that direction." Effective immediately, Mr Trudeau stated only elected members of the House of Commons would serve in the

Liberal caucus and that the thirty-two Liberals sitting in the Senate would no longer be part of his parliamentary team.[1] His statement was bold and unprecedented.

Two events characterize the background to Mr Trudeau's announcement: the unsuccessful efforts of the previous government to bring change to the Senate, and the 2012–13 expenses scandal.

Shortly after the election of the Conservative government in 2006, Prime Minister Stephen Harper appeared before the Special Senate Committee on Senate Reform declaring:

> [T]he Senate must change, and we intend to make it happen. The government is not looking for another report — it is seeking action … Such reform will make the Senate more democratic, more accountable and more in keeping with the expectations of Canadians who, as we all know, are not at all satisfied with the status quo.[2]

During its mandate, Mr Harper's government introduced a number of reform bills, including S-4, *Constitution Act, 2006 (Senate tenure)*, by which senators would serve eight-year terms; and C-20, the *Senate Appointment Consultations Act*, and C-7, the *Senate Reform Act*, which would set frameworks for consultative elections of nominees for Senate office.[3] His administration proceeded with the proposed legislation because it believed "Parliament can act, without engaging other levels of government in a complex constitutional discussion or amendment process."[4] Bill C-7 was subsequently challenged by the Quebec government in the Quebec Court of Appeal and found to be unconstitutional.

The government then referred a series of questions to the Supreme Court, including whether it is within the legislative authority of Parliament to make changes for fixed terms, and whether Parliament had the competence to enact legislation that provides a means of consulting Canadians as to its preferences for potential nominees for appointment to the Senate. At the time Mr Trudeau issued his statement, the Court had not yet delivered its opinion.

Regarding the expenses scandal, throughout late 2012 and early 2013, questions had arisen about the living and travel expenses of certain senators, which resulted in the Senate's Internal Economy, Budgets, and Administration Committee ordering independent audits of their expense claims. In June 2013, Senator Marjorie LeBreton, the leader of the government in the Senate, presented a motion requesting the auditor general to conduct a comprehensive audit of Senate expenses, including senators' expenses, which was adopted by the Senate on 6 June 2013. J Patrick Boyer observed: "The Senate expenses scandal obsessed Canadians and sent our parliamentary life spinning down an unfamiliar path."[5]

CES Franks notes that Senate reform proposals are divided into two distinct camps: "The first, smaller group consists of those concerned with improving the existing Senate. The second consists of reforms tied in with questions of the federal system in Canada and its weaknesses."[6]

Mr Trudeau's changes fell within the first group. Others had proposed changing the appointment method. In 1972, a special joint committee (Molgat-MacGuigan) observed:

> The method of selection of Senators has been much open to criticism. Many Canadians think of Senate appointments (made, in fact if not in form, by the Prime Minister) as simply a method of rewarding party faithful. With all due respect to the many fine appointments which have been made, there have been over the years too many appointments which in the eyes of the public confirm this view. The system of appointment is therefore suspect … If the Senate is to fulfill properly its role, the criterion for membership must not be reward for past service, but rather the *expectation of future service to the nation, based on a recognition of ability and past service in various fields of endeavour.*

In contrast to Trudeau's proposal, Molgat-MacGuigan did not propose doing away with partisan appointments:

> This is not to say that political appointments are wrong per se — after all, the Senate is part of the political structure; it is a political arena. The criticism is not that politicians are appointed, but rather the reason for their appointment.[7]

Likewise, the 2000 Wakeham Commission on the reform of the House of Lords also recommended against a non-partisan upper house. It believed a reformed House of Lords,

> whatever precise form it takes, will inevitably be a political chamber. Some of our witnesses and a number of those who wrote to us seemed to imagine that the new second chamber should be, and could be, a sort of council of tribal elders; a body of wise men and women capable of determining, in a wholly detached manner and in the light of an entirely dispassionate examination of all the available evidence, what was in the nation's best interests. Such a vision is, in our view, pure fantasy. Politics exists because people disagree, often passionately. The new second chamber, like the old, will be and should be one of the principal forums in which these disagreements are expressed ... (T)he new second chamber, like any other legislative chamber, will require a degree of discipline and organisation ... (P)olitical parties will continue to have ... a central role to play. The new second chamber will be a political body, and practical politics requires political parties.[8]

The Supreme Court's View of the Senate and 2014 Opinion

In its April 2014 answer to the reference given to the Court concerning the reform of the Senate, the Supreme Court concluded that the goal of the Fathers of Confederation was that senators provide "sober second thought" and function with independence when conducting legislative review. It stated the Senate had historically attracted criticism that "it failed to provide 'sober second thought' and reflected the same partisan spirit as the House of Commons."[9] Reaffirming an earlier opinion expressed in the 1980 *Upper House Reference*,[10] the Court held:

> [T]he intention was to make the Senate a thoroughly independent body which would canvass dispassionately the measures of the

House of Commons … The framers sought to endow the Senate with independence from the electoral process to which members of the House of Commons were subject, in order to remove Senators from a partisan political arena that required unremitting consideration of short-term political objectives.[11]

The Court defined the architecture of the Senate as a "complementary body of sober second thought," repeating the point eleven times.[12] "The framers of the *Constitution Act, 1867* deliberately chose executive appointment of Senators in order to allow the Senate to play the specific role of a complementary legislative body."[13] The second chamber was not to be "a perennial rival of the House of Commons in the legislative process."

> Appointed Senators would not have a popular mandate — they would not have the expectations and legitimacy that stem from popular election. This would ensure that they confine themselves to their role as a body mainly conducting legislative review, rather than as a coequal of the House of Commons.[14]

Regarding the Harper reforms, the Court concluded: "Parliament and the provinces are equal stakeholders in the Canadian constitutional design. Neither level of government acting alone can alter the fundamental nature and role of the institutions provided for in the Constitution."[15] Changing Senate tenure and implementing consultative elections would need provincial consent.[16]

The Non-partisan, Complementary Senate

The newly formed Trudeau government opted for changing the composition of the Senate as opposed to its constitutional roles. Donald Savoie feels Trudeau "could do little else, given the country's regional diversity and interests, the rigidity of our constitution, and the Supreme Court ruling."[17] By moving to a system of non-partisan appointments, the government believed its performance as a complementary body would be strengthened.[18]

It created an advisory board to provide non-binding, merit-based recommendations to the prime minister on Senate nominations. Consisting of three federal members and two persons chosen from each of the provinces where a vacancy is to be filled, the board established criteria for recommending senators, such as gender, Indigenous, and minority balance; a solid knowledge of the legislative process and the Constitution, "including the role of the Senate as an independent and complementary body of sober second thought, regional representation and minority representation"; and personal qualities such as ethics and integrity. It also stressed that individuals demonstrate they have "the ability to bring a perspective and contribution to the work of the Senate that is independent and non-partisan."[19]

Professor Savoie, who served as a member of the advisory board from New Brunswick, wrote that his experience was positive:

> The process worked as it was intended. I did not see or feel any interference from the political level. All Canadians were free to apply, and our deliberations were held in a non-partisan and professional way. If there were a bias, it was against former politicians, including Liberal ones … We were asked to submit five names for every vacancy and in all cases the prime minister selected from the five names. It was made clear that the prime minister would decide, and that he may or may not consult ministers.[20]

Impact of Mr Trudeau's Reforms

Since taking office in 2015, the government has appointed several senators from a variety of professions and backgrounds. The Senate's composition has been positively altered with gender parity being achieved in late 2020, a remarkable accomplishment for any parliamentary institution. Its workways have changed. The senators appointed by Prime Minister Trudeau form the backbone of the Independent Senators Group (ISG), whose members are unaffiliated with any political caucus and work cooperatively with each other but act independently. David E Smith feels senators have now been "freed of the partisan chains that linked them for a century and a half to the House of Commons." They could turn their attention to improving legislation and not thwarting government, take up popular causes, and "undertake a new role as an ally of the people."[21] Several recent committee reports appear to bear this out.[22]

In September 2018, the Institute for Research on Public Policy (IRPP) held a roundtable discussion on the Trudeau reforms that was attended by senators, academics, government officials, and Senate staff. The roundtable noted:

> Ministers can no longer rely on a block of senators from the same camp, and often have to get involved earlier in the legislative process, including providing briefings to smaller groups of senators. Because they are examining legislation more closely, senators are calling more often on senior officials to provide technical expertise. In some cases, senior officials have even briefed individual senators.[23]

There was much praise for the way the Senate reviewed Bill C-45, the legalization of cannabis. Detailed scrutiny was given by five Senate committees that heard from more than 240 witnesses and eight appearances by ministers. The debate on third reading lasted for six sittings, organized around themes, with a deadline for terminating the debate agreed to in advance.

The roundtable also commented positively on the innovation of having Cabinet ministers participate in the Senate Question Period:

> Previously, the government leader in the Senate, who was usually also a member of the cabinet, responded to questions on the full range of issues. Now, the government representative in the Senate is not a minister, and cannot speak for the government. The Senate therefore initiated the practice of inviting a minister to participate in Question Period, usually once every sitting week. The selection of ministers is done in consultation with all caucuses and groups of senators, and the scheduling is coordinated by the government representative.[24]

However, the renewed Senate still faces challenges. Emmett Macfarlane feels the reforms have made the legislative process more complex:

> One of the most significant challenges the government has had in getting its legislative agenda through the second chamber has been organizational: with the majority of senators no longer in a party caucus, the benefits of getting large groups of senators "on the same page" have been lost.[25]

Removing political parties from the legislative process is not without consequences. One of the key functions of political parties is to aggregate interests, allowing the decision-making process to become more manageable. On one occasion, the Senate placed a great number of amendments on the public record. For example, in 2019, in its study of C-69, a quite technical bill, the Energy, Environment, and Natural Resources Committee reported over 180 amendments. In total, nearly 230 amendments were agreed to by the Senate and sent to the House of Commons for its concurrence.[26]

Bicameralism requires each house to deliberate on the changes to legislative proposals sent to them from the other chamber. Senate amendments to Commons bills are meant for the consideration not just of the sponsoring minister and Cabinet but for all the members of the House, as well as the general public. Returning Bill C-69 to the other place with so many amendments made it difficult to discern what the Senate's priorities were. The new Senate may need to augment its legislative effectiveness by finding a system to better aggregate and prioritize amendments. Including in its message to the House of Commons a narrative of the Senate's position on a bill may be an alternative procedure.

Writing in 2018, David E Smith said: "[I]t is difficult to make an absolute judgment as to whether this development (the non-partisan, emerging Senate) is good or bad for Canadian politics."[27] It appears, however, the new Senate's competency and commitment to public service is without question. Clearly, the increased activity and interactions of senators in the legislative process have revived

Canadian bicameralism and negated the torpid stereotype of "sleeping" or "absent" senators.

What is unclear is whether removing partisanship has significantly altered the Senate's review of legislation. Despite the past nature of appointments, the Senate has always exhibited a broad capacity to study legislation both in the chamber and committee. The new Senate may only be continuing a long-established role.

While final assessments are premature, the revived Senate may have weakened the effectiveness of its other two bicameral models. Its capacity to act as a sort of institutional ombudsman in the Canadian parliamentary system, as it did in the Coyne Affair in 1961, may be impacted. As well, its primary focus on legislative review may have restricted its role of regional representation. At the 2019 IRPP roundtable, Professor Jennifer Wallner reported she had reviewed all the Senate committee reports issued during the previous year and did not find a single reference to regional implications.[28]

The Need for Further Reform

The new Senate has not escaped its deeper, structural problems. The issue of representation, which Roger Gibbins, a past president of the Canada West Foundation, once said goes "to the very core of the Senate ... who we should represent and what are the means of representation,"[29] remains to be addressed. The question of the appropriate allocation of seats to Western provinces has not been resolved. The broad legislative power the Senate possesses continues to lack a democratic basis. Even though the Senate is a public institution, senators remain unaccountable to Canadians while serving to the age of seventy-five. Notwithstanding Mr Trudeau's commitment to change the process that saw senators "appointed by one person, and one person only," the special prerogative of the prime minister to make recommendations for the appointment of senators is still in place.[30] The numerous provisions of the *Constitution Act, 1867*, which no longer serve a public purpose — the age, property, and citizenship provisions, and those relating to bankruptcy and infamous crimes — continue. The lack of formal representation of the inhabitants of Nunavik in northern Quebec still exists. As well, Canadians remain excluded from parliamentary discussions of how to modernize the Senate for twenty-first century Canada.

The road to a redesign of the Senate's architecture lies in federal–provincial negotiations, as well as the competency of the Parliament of Canada itself. The prospects for structural reform to again make the Senate a force for unity within the country, as it was in 1867, will be the subject of our final chapter.

CHAPTER EIGHT

Prospects for Structural Reform

In *Reference re Senate Reform, 2014*, the Supreme Court concluded that term limits for senators and consultative elections for their nomination fall under the general amending procedure, namely section 38(1) of the *Constitution Act, 1982*. This process requires the consent of Parliament and at least seven provinces representing at least 50 percent of the Canadian population. As former Senator Hugh Segal noted: "For better or worse, the court's decision reflected precisely what the Fathers of Confederation had actually designed." Their agreement on the Senate "was not some slapdash last-minute compromise" but rather "the resulting embrace of balance and compromise."[1] Structural reform requires substantial provincial consent.

The Court was commenting specifically about those proposals that "engage the interests of the provinces." It noted that section 38(1) was not the only amending formula that could bring constitutional change to the Senate. It highlighted section 44, which states that Parliament "may exclusively make laws amending the Constitution of Canada in relation to the executive government of Canada or the Senate or the House of Commons." The Court added: "Section 44, as an exception to the general procedure, encompasses measures that maintain or change the Senate without altering its fundamental nature and role."[2]

The justices felt the requirement that senators have a personal net worth of at least $4,000 could be repealed under section 44, since "it updates the constitutional framework relating to the Senate without affecting the institution's fundamental nature and role."[3] Former Senate Speaker Dan Hays has observed there are other sections of the *Constitution Act, 1867* that could also be modernized under section 44.

One example is section 23(1), the provision that requires a senator to be at least thirty years of age. Hays feels the section could be replaced by a statement that a senator be a qualified elector, that is be at least eighteen years old. Regarding section 31(2), that a seat must be vacated if a senator becomes a dual citizen, Hays notes:

> [W]hen the *Constitution Act, 1867* was drafted, the concept of citizenship was considerably different than it is today. The idea of dual citizenship did not exist, as the assumption was that you could be loyal to only one country at a time. As we know, a person can acquire citizenship in another country without applying or doing any positive act. For instance, in some cases, by marrying a citizen of a particular country, one automatically becomes a citizen of that country. If there are circumstances in which dual citizenship is allowed under the laws of Canada, it should not be an impediment to Senate membership as it is not now an impediment to membership in the House of Commons.[4]

Likewise, there is a need to modernize section 31(4), which specifies the seat of a senator attainted of treason or convicted of felony, or of any infamous crime, be vacated. Hays observes:

> The crime of treason is still in the *Criminal Code* although very rarely invoked. The word has been contentious in Canadian history, and should perhaps be removed. The concepts of felonies and misdemeanours were replaced in the original *Code* by indictable offenses and summary conviction offences. Generally speaking, in 1867 felonies were graver crimes perhaps punishable by death which resulted in the forfeiture of the perpetrator's lands

and goods to the Crown. The word felony should be replaced by "indictable offence".[5]

These are some provisions that the federal Parliament could unilaterally amend to improve the quality of governance. However, there has been a reluctance to initiate such action. There is even greater hesitation to move on substantial reform in conjunction with the provinces. There is certainly no shortage of ideas. What constitutional amendments have been proposed in the recent past, and the impediments they faced, is the subject of our next section.

The 1960–1990 Period

Beginning in the 1960s, Senate reform became a salient political issue. Responding to the pressures of the Quiet Revolution in Quebec and resentments in Western Canada, numerous efforts were made to alter the Senate's design. They included detailed white papers, extensive committee studies, proposed bills, and the appointment of commissions. Some came from the federal arena and others from the provincial arenas. Their themes, which will be discussed below, focused on perceived Senate shortcomings, namely improving federalism, a more equitable redistribution of seats, Indigenous peoples' representation, changing the power relationship with the House of Commons, and proposals for electing senators. The following are the most important reports released by the Senate during this period:

- The 1968 statement of policy by the Government of Canada, *Federalism for the Future*
- The 1969 White Paper, *The Constitution and the People of Canada*
- The 1972 report of the Special Joint Committee of the Senate and of the House of Commons on the Constitution of Canada (Molgat-MacGuigan)
- The *Constitutional Amendment Bill* (C-60) tabled by the PE Trudeau government in 1978
- *Reform of the Canadian Senate* published in 1978 by the Government of British Columbia

- The 1979 Task Force on Canadian Unity, *A Future Together — Observations and Recommendations* (Pepin-Robarts)
- The 1984 report of the Special Joint Committee of the Senate and of the House of Commons on Senate Reform (Molgat-Cosgrove)
- The 1985 report of the *Royal Commission of the Economic Union and Development Prospects for Canada,* Volume 3 (Macdonald Commission)
- The 1985 report of the Alberta Select Special Committee on Senate Reform
- The 1992 report of the Special Joint Committee of the Senate and of the House of Commons on a Renewed Canada (Beaudoin-Dobbie)
- *Consensus Report on the Constitution: Final Text*, Charlottetown, August 28, 1992 (Charlottetown Accord)[6]

Improving Federalism and the Redistribution of Seats

Reformers focused largely on improving regional representation. For example, British Columbia's *Reform of the Canadian Senate* proposed that the Senate be replaced by a variation of the German Bundesrat, probably the most territorially based upper chamber in the world, in which members would be appointed by provincial governments and act on their instructions.[7] Pepin-Robarts also recommended a Bundesrat-style Senate composed of appointees of provincial governments where there would be "power brokerage operations between the two orders of government."[8]

They also recommended changing the allotment of seats. Molgat-MacGuigan, Bill C-60, Molgat-Cosgrove, the Macdonald Commission, and the Alberta Select Committee all suggested a new seat distribution. Their advice varied. Pepin-Robarts argued the Senate should have only sixty seats, while Molgat-Cosgrove and the Macdonald Commission believed its size could be increased to 144.[9]

They also proposed equality of seats. The Alberta Select Committee felt the Senate should "maintain as its primary purpose the objective established by the Fathers of Confederation, namely, to represent the regions."[10] It recommended each province have six seats, the same number of seats Alberta already had. The Charlottetown Accord also proposed six seats for each province with the Northwest Territories and the Yukon each receiving one.[11]

Indigenous Peoples Representation

Making the Senate a forum in which Indigenous peoples are given greater parliamentary representation was also included. Under the Charlottetown Accord, a unanimous effort was made by all first ministers to modernize the character of Canadian federalism while better reconciling with the people of Canada's First Nations. The Accord's Consensus Report recommended:

> Aboriginal representation in the Senate should be guaranteed in the Constitution. Aboriginal Senate seats should be additional to provincial and territorial seats, rather than drawn from any province or territory's allocation of Senate seats.
>
> Aboriginal Senators should have the same role and powers as other Senators, plus a possible double majority power in relation to certain matters materially affecting Aboriginal people. These issues and other details relating to Aboriginal representation in the Senate (numbers, distribution, method of selection) will be discussed further by governments and the representatives of the Aboriginal Peoples in the early autumn of 1992.[12]

With the defeat of the Charlottetown Accord in a national referendum held on 26 October 1992, the proposals were not acted upon.

Altering the Power Arrangement with the House of Commons

Suggestions were also made to limit the Senate's powers. Jack Stilborn notes:

Most of these proposals argue that these powers would enable the Senate to be more effective, while at the same time preventing it from being so powerful that it could deadlock the legislative process or complicate the practice of responsible government.[13]

Molgat-MacGuigan recommended the Senate have a suspensive veto for six months, while Bill C-60 proposed sixty days for ordinary legislation. Pepin-Robarts felt the approval of the upper house would not even be required for legislation within exclusive federal jurisdiction. Molgat-Cosgrove believed the Senate should have a veto of up to 120 sitting days on all legislation except supply bills, which would not be subject to any delay. The Alberta Select Committee proposed 180 days over constitutional amendments and ninety days over money or taxation bills. The Macdonald Commission recommended a suspensive veto of six months on all ordinary legislation but an absolute veto over measures having special linguistic significance.

The Charlottetown Accord recommended distinctions between classes of legislation. For example, the Senate would have the power to delay ordinary legislation for up to thirty sitting days; to delay revenue and expenditure bills also for up to thirty calendar days; to amend or defeat, by means of a double majority of both all senators and francophone senators, bills materially affecting French language or culture; and to amend or defeat bills involving fundamental tax policy changes directly related to natural resources. The Accord also suggested the use of joint sittings of the Senate and the House of Commons as a procedure to determine the fate of most bills.

Proposals for an Elected Senate

That senators be selected by using another model of bicameralism — the popular sovereignty model that the Fathers rejected but remained part of the historical family of Canadian bicameralism — was also proposed. Molgat-Cosgrove argued that an elected Senate would have more political authority. The Alberta Select

Committee stated that only a directly elected Senate "would enjoy legitimacy and would be able to exercise fully the significant political and legislative powers necessary to make a valuable contribution to the Canadian Parliament." The Macdonald Commission felt "the Senate is part of Parliament, and Parliament is pre-eminently a representative body. For that reason ... we join those who have argued that the Senate should be an elected body."[14]

The Charlottetown Accord also recommended an elected Senate, with some senators being directly elected and others indirectly:

> The Constitution should be amended to provide that Senators are elected, either by the population of the provinces and territories of Canada or by the members of their provincial or territorial legislative assemblies.
>
> Federal legislation should govern elections, subject to the constitutional provision above and constitutional provisions requiring that elections take place at the same time as elections to the House of Commons and provisions respecting eligibility and mandate of Senators. Federal legislation would be sufficiently flexible to allow provinces and territories to provide for gender equality in the composition of the Senate.
>
> Matters should be expedited in order that Senate elections be held as soon as possible, and, if feasible, at the same time as the next federal general election for the House of Commons.[15]

The Failure of Structural Reform

As Jack Stilborn has observed: "Discussion of Senate reform has been a near-constant feature of the Canadian political landscape over the past forty years ... All of the proposals ended in failure."[16] Donald Savoie feels: "When it comes to the Senate, Canada is like a deer caught in the headlights; Canadians know they need to reform the Senate but they simply cannot get it done."[17] Danielle Pinard speculates that the Senate may be condemned to survive unchanged.[18] Many reasons have been advanced for why substantial reform has failed.

David E Smith feels structural reform could diminish the Senate's independent judgment on legislation and threaten the benefits a complementary model provides:

> Canada is one of the world's most stable and democratic political systems. A contributing factor to this end has been the adaptive and accommodative capacity of its institutions. In this respect the Senate has played an important part.... As a working institution, however, it is seldom criticized. On the contrary, its committees are praised for their skill and diligence. It is ironic, therefore, that reforms advanced for the Senate often threaten to diminish the contribution the present structure makes to the quality of parliamentary legislation.[19]

Others feel strengthening the Senate, especially through a system of elections, would be incompatible with the Westminster system and jeopardize responsible government. Bruce M Hicks and André Blais conclude electing the Senate "would have a transformative effect on its legitimacy and powers." Parliament could be gripped in deadlock as the Senate would not hesitate to use its full range of powers. The role of the House of Commons as the confidence chamber would likely be threatened. Senators would lose their independence, their "sober second thought," and long-term vision.[20]

Likewise, many have been troubled by proposals that call for the equality of provincial seats. Gordon Robertson believed that such an arrangement would be a mistake: "Quebec could not be cut down from 25 per cent to 10 per cent when it contained 80 per cent of the French-speaking population of Canada."[21] David E Smith writes that a Triple E proposal (elected, equal, and effective)

> remains a little constitutional image. Too much is left out; for example, Triple E has nothing to say to Quebec or First Nations ... How will the new Senate work with the House of Commons? What provision will there be for breaking deadlocks ... How well will the symmetrical Senate the Triple E system proposes serve Canada's asymmetrical federalism?[22]

Above all, Senate reform is not a straightforward issue. Its reform would be linked to other constitutional changes. Jennifer Smith observes:

> The Senate is a central institution ... But it is not a stand-alone institution. If it changes, its relationships with other institutions — the House of Commons, the Cabinet, the Crown, the provinces — will change as well. That's the trouble with Senate reform. It is actually a very big issue with complex ramifications for the conduct of Canadian politics.[23]

The strategies and tactics employed have also been problematic. Initiatives that avoided formal engagement with the provinces or public consultation have ended in failure. The Trudeau government's unilateral attempt to reform the Senate in 1978 with Bill C-60 was found to be unconstitutional. The Harper government's bills on term limits and consultative elections experienced a similar fate. The Mulroney government's *1984 Powers of the Senate Amendment* was tabled in the House of Commons without public discussion and was shortly abandoned.[24]

Mega-constitutional initiatives, such as the Charlottetown Accord, have also proved unsuccessful. The Accord encompassed several issues, such as the right of Indigenous peoples to self-government, Quebec as a distinct society, and Senate reform. Negotiating a successful agreement meant concessions and parliamentary trade-offs. Ty Ludwig writes that the Accord was "a conglomeration of compromises by the many different parties involved in negotiating it."

> Western Canada resoundingly voted against the Charlottetown Accord and a major factor of this result lay in the concessions for a reformed senate. Western Canada had been negotiating for better regional representation and had looked to a "Triple E" senate as a solution ... Westerners had many problems with the concessions made in order to achieve a consensus such as granting the Provinces the choice as to how to choose their senators ... In actuality, "the boosts given were small ..." Combine this with the fact that

the Senate would only hold a limited veto, thereby undermining its "effective" status; ... it is not hard to make a connection between the concessions the Charlottetown Accord made and the vote results in British Columbia and Alberta.[25]

The agreement reached in the Accord awarded 25 percent of House of Commons seats to Quebec in exchange for an equal Senate of six seats per province. Gordon Robertson saw this provision as contributing to its defeat:

A second chamber in a federal system is supposed to be a balancing factor: to offset the domination of the "lower chamber," where representation is by population, by the populous centres of Canada. Quebec was one of the populous areas; it shared control with Ontario of the House of Commons. It did not need any guarantee of membership there. The Quebec guarantee became a major target of criticism in the rest of Canada.[26]

Prospects for New Initiatives

The issue of fundamental Senate reform remains clouded in pessimism. It continues to be portrayed as a pointless debate that distracts from other issues. Cross-party cooperation to bring forth new proposals does not exist. Despite the importance of the issue, Senate reform is not a national priority. Peter McCormick has stated: "[T]he growth of an elected Senate would be at least as much at the cost of the future pretensions of premiers as it would be at the cost of the national government or the House of Commons."[27] Meg Russell writes:

[T]he government and House of Commons have nothing to gain from Senate reform, and everything to lose. It is accepted that a reformed Senate, particularly one which is elected, would no longer be frightened to make full use of its powers. Even if the formal powers of the Senate were reduced, this could still create more problems for the governing party than a notionally powerful but unconfident appointed chamber. Thus there is no pressure from the top to push through the proposals once they are made, or to draw the perpetual Senate reform debate to an end.[28]

Notwithstanding this mood of pessimism, the importance of renewing one of this country's foundational political institutions and ushering it into the twenty-first century persists. New initiatives may find greater success if the question of reform was once again put forward as one of national unity and the benefits it could convey to the Canadian polity. The original compact on the Senate brought the country together. Without it, George Brown said, "we could not have advanced one step." There are far too few Canadian institutions that can contribute to national integration. As former Senator Michael Pitfield noted, the Senate has a unique role to play.[29] Political elites as well as the Canadian public might become more engaged in finding solutions if repairing the Senate also included how a reformed Senate can lessen the country's divisions and improve governance. National unity should never be seen as a distraction.

The recommendations of the 1960–90 period often made this point. For example, the 1969 White Paper, *The Constitution and the People of Canada*, stated:

The Government of Canada feels the Senate should be reorganized to provide for the expression in it, in a more direct and formal manner than at present, of the interests of the provinces. At the same time, the interests of the country as a whole should continue to find expression in the Senate to maintain there an influence for the unity of Canada.[30]

Molgat-MacGuigan made a similar suggestion:

The reasons which prompted the Fathers of Confederation to set up a bicameral legislative process in Canada are still valid today. Federal states in particular have found upper houses valuable. They allow greater regional representation at the level of central government. The federal legislative process can and does benefit from regional representation.

The importance of this role cannot be denied. The problems of regional disparities, the recurring talk of alienation from some regions, of separatism from others, and the concern about domination by the Central Provinces reinforce traditional and theoretical arguments. The growth and development of Canada has not reduced regionalism in some aspects, but has rather enhanced it as regions grew stronger. Much remains to be done to improve the relations and understanding between regions, and the Senate can be one important tool.[31]

While it is possible that the problematic components of the Senate's design will be abandoned and it will emerge as a single-purpose house, like the complementary House of Lords or a fully elected one like the American Senate, such action will be at odds with Canada's history and tradition. Most of the major proposals of the 1960s–90s did not aim at creating a "new" upper house but attempted to modernize its original multi-purpose function. The recommendations for improving federalism through a redistribution of Senate seats, altering the powers of the Senate, and proposing greater representation for Indigenous peoples focused on updating the original framework to provide more effective parliamentary government. Admittedly, another model was added — the popular sovereignty model — but one not totally at odds with Canadian bicameralism.

For example, the Charlottetown Accord redesigned all three bicameral models. It strengthened the territorial component by recommending seats be distributed based on provincial equality. The mixed government model, although weakened, would remain, in that the Senate would be influential over some types of legislation, specifically bills affecting the French language and culture and tax policy changes related to natural resources. As well, the Senate would be given new powers to ratify key appointments. The complementary model would be better defined as revenue and expenditure bills would be subject to a thirty-day suspensive veto. If a bill was defeated or amended by the Senate within this period, it could be repassed by a simple majority in the House of Commons. The first ministers also revitalized the fourth model of the Canadian bicameral family by proposing that senators be elected either directly by the people or by the provincial legislatures.

The Charlottetown Accord was defeated in a national referendum, but this should not pose a final barrier to further discussion of how a reformed Senate could better accommodate national interests. Improved initiatives might look like these:

1) A revised territorial model, with seats being allocated to largest, middle-sized, and smaller provinces, or establishing an adaptive formula allowing seat allocations to vary as conditions change.[32] Clearly, Quebec's territorial representation needs modernizing to ensure Nunavik in northern Quebec is formally represented.

2) Further revising the territorial model to ensure a greater dimension of Canadian diversity is represented. That would include guaranteeing Indigenous peoples representation in the Senate. The Truth and Reconciliation Commission believed that reconciliation is about establishing a mutually respectful relationship between Indigenous and non-Indigenous peoples. Allowing for the selection of a fixed number of Indigenous senators through a consultative or direct election process would be an important gesture not only for advancing reconciliation in Canada but for the reform of the Senate itself. Such a guarantee will provide Indigenous peoples a means to partner in the governance of Canada and acknowledge their distinct interests, cultures, and values. Proposals in this regard would require the consent of Indigenous peoples.

3) Strengthening the Senate's powers as a balancing factor to offset regional disparities. The challenge will be to convince provincial and territorial leaders that a reformed Senate will not pose a threat to their governments.

4) Developing alternative designs for an elected Senate, including a mixed composition of elected and non-elected members. Consideration should be given to using an electoral system based on the single transferrable vote (STV), which allows voters to

rank their preferences for candidates. Term limits should be included.

5) Revising the mixed government model as a requirement of modern government in Canada. Professor Franks noted, "the role of the Senate must be clarified, because the more you move toward an elected Senate and one that has, in a sense, more legitimacy, the more the procedural rules must be clarified as to when the Senate can use its powers."[33] Former Senate Speaker Dan Hays believes that in any reformed system "the primary role of the House of Commons must be maintained as its members will accept nothing less." Hays adds, however, "It would be unfortunate if the Senate's powers were too severely curbed. Restrictions, such as giving the Senate a relatively short suspensive veto on legislation or removing its right to deal effectively with tax or borrowing authority legislation, would hinder the Senate. They would limit the ability of senators to represent national and provincial interests or act as an important check on the executive."[34]

6) Ensuring the grant of supply to the Crown is the sole gift of the House of Commons. The Senate would only examine and make recommendations on the provisions of appropriation bills. The conventions of responsible government would remain intact.

7) Protecting the effectiveness of the complementary model. The present Senate workways that allow senators more time to devote to legislative and committee studies, their lack of restrictive procedures, and their *independent mind set* should be encouraged.[35] Senators should be constitutionally excluded from being a member of the Cabinet or any of its committees.

Finding the political leadership and will needed to address the issue within a federal–provincial setting will not be easy, but given its importance, not impossible. New initiatives should be framed in terms of making Canada stronger. They must include all-party discussions; committed dialogue with individual Canadians, interested groups, stakeholders, Indigenous peoples; and, of course, negotiations with the provinces and territories. Such discussions should not be restricted by self-imposed timelines. The appointment of a royal commission may assist in finding a new path to structural reform.

To modernize the Canadian Senate for the twenty-first century, the previous proposals for reform should be re-examined in terms of how they came up short and their impact on other institutions of government. As Jack Stilborn notes: "[T]he value of these proposals, as a 'resource base' that can, and should, be given close attention by future proponents of reform speaks for itself."[36] Not surprisingly, any finalized redesigned second chamber will be the outcome of negotiation and compromise, which characterizes so much of Canadian politics.

Selected Extracts Relating to the Senate in the *Constitution Act, 1867*

IV. Legislative Power

Constitution of Parliament of Canada

17 There shall be One Parliament for Canada, consisting of the Queen, an Upper House styled the Senate, and the House of Commons.

Privileges, etc. of Houses

18 The privileges, immunities, and powers to be held, enjoyed, and exercised by the Senate and by the House of Commons, and by the members thereof respectively, shall be such as are from time to time defined by Act of the Parliament of Canada, but so that any Act of the Parliament of Canada defining such privileges, immunities, and powers shall not confer any privileges, immunities, and powers exceeding those at the passing of such Act held, enjoyed, and exercised by the Commons House of Parliament of the United Kingdom of Great Britain and Ireland, and by the members thereof.

The Senate

Number of Senators

21 The Senate shall, subject to the Provisions of this Act, consist of One Hundred and five Members, who shall be styled Senators.

Representation of Provinces in Senate

22 In relation to the Constitution of the Senate Canada shall be deemed to consist of *Four* Divisions:–

1. Ontario;
2. Quebec;
3. The Maritime Provinces, Nova Scotia and New Brunswick, and Prince Edward Island;
4. The Western Provinces of Manitoba, British Columbia, Saskatchewan, and Alberta;

which Four Divisions shall (subject to the Provisions of this Act) be equally represented in the Senate as follows: Ontario by twenty-four senators; Quebec by twenty-four senators; the Maritime Provinces and Prince Edward Island by twenty-four senators, ten thereof representing Nova Scotia, ten thereof representing New Brunswick, and four thereof representing Prince Edward Island; the Western Provinces by twenty-four senators, six thereof representing Manitoba, six thereof representing British Columbia, six thereof representing Saskatchewan, and six thereof representing Alberta; Newfoundland shall be entitled to be represented in the Senate by six members; the Yukon Territory, the Northwest Territories, and Nunavut shall be entitled to be represented in the Senate by one member each.

In the Case of Quebec each of the Twenty-four Senators representing that Province shall be appointed for One of the Twenty-four Electoral Divisions of Lower Canada specified in Schedule A to Chapter One of the Consolidated Statutes of Canada.

Qualifications of Senator

23 The Qualifications of a Senator shall be as follows:

1. He shall be of the full age of Thirty Years;
2. He shall be either a natural-born Subject of the Queen, or a Subject of the Queen naturalized by an Act of the Parliament of Great Britain, or the Parliament of Great Britain and Ireland, or of the Legislature of One of the Provinces of Upper Canada,

Lower Canada, Canada, Nova Scotia, or New Brunswick, before the Union, or the Parliament of Canada after the Union;

3. He shall be legally or equitably seised as of Freehold for his own Use and Benefit of Lands or Tenements held in Free and Common Socage, or seised or possessed for his own Use and Benefit of Lands or Tenements held in Franc-alleu or in Roture, within the Province for which he is appointed, of the Value of Four thousand Dollars, over and above all Rents, Dues, Debts, Charges, Mortgages, and Incumbrances due or payable out of or charged on or affecting the same;

4. His Real and Personal Property shall be together worth Four thousand Dollars over and above his Debts and Liabilities;

5, He shall be resident in the Province for which he is appointed;

6. In the Case of Quebec he shall have his Real Property Qualification in the Electoral Division for which he is appointed, or shall be resident in that Division.

Summons of Senator

24 The Governor General shall from Time to Time, in the Queen's name, by Instrument under the Great Seal of Canada, summon qualified Persons to the Senate; and, subject to the Provisions of this Act, every Person so summoned shall become and be a Member of the Senate and a Senator.

25 Such persons shall be first summoned to the Senate as the Queen by Warrant under Her Majesty's Royal Sign Manual thinks fit to approve, and their Names shall be inserted in the Queen's Proclamation of Union. [Repealed].

Addition of Senators in certain cases

26 If at any Time on the Recommendation of the Governor General the Queen thinks fit to direct that Four or Eight Members be added to the Senate, the Governor General may by Summons to Four or Eight qualified Persons (as the Case may be), representing equally the Four Divisions of Canada, add to the Senate accordingly.

Reduction of Senate to normal Number

27 In case of such Addition being at any Time made, the Governor General shall not summon any Person to the Senate, except on a further like Direction by the Queen on the like Recommendation, to represent one of the Four Divisions until such Division is represented by Twenty-four Senators and no more.

Maximum Number of Senators

28 The Number of Senators shall not at any Time exceed One Hundred and twelve.

Tenure of Place in Senate

29(1) Subject to subsection (2), a Senator shall, subject to the provisions of this Act, hold his place in the Senate for life.

(2) A Senator who is summoned to the Senate after the coming into force of this subsection shall, subject to this Act, hold his place in the Senate until he attains the age of seventy-five years.

Resignation of Place in Senate

30 A Senator may by Writing under his Hand addressed to the Governor General resign his Place in the Senate, and thereupon the same shall be vacant.

Disqualification of Senators

31 The Place of a Senator shall become vacant in any of the following Cases:

1. If for Two consecutive Sessions in the Parliament he fails to give his Attendance in the Senate;
2. If he takes an Oath or makes a Declaration or Acknowledgement of Allegiance, Obedience, or Adherence to a Foreign Power, or does an Act whereby he becomes a Subject or Citizen, or entitled to the Rights or Privileges of a Subject or Citizen, of a Foreign Power;
3. If he is adjudged Bankrupt or Insolvent, or applies for the Benefit of any Law relating to Insolvent Debtors, or becomes a public Defaulter;

4. If he is attainted of Treason or convicted of Felony or of any
    infamous Crime;

5. If he ceases to be qualified in respect of Property or of Residence;
    provided, that a Senator shall not be deemed to have ceased to
    be qualified in respect of Residence by reason only of his resid-
    ing at the Seat of the Government of Canada while holding an
    Office under that Government requiring his Presence there.

Summons on Vacancy in Senate

32 When a Vacancy happens in the Senate by Resignation, Death,
or otherwise, the Governor General shall by Summons to a fit and
qualified Person fill the Vacancy.

Questions as to Qualifications and Vacancies in Senate

33 If any Question arises respecting the Qualification of a Senator
or a Vacancy in the Senate the same shall be heard and determined
by the Senate.

Appointment of Speaker of Senate

34 The Governor General may from Time to Time, by Instrument
under the Great Seal of Canada, appoint a Senator to be Speaker of
the Senate, and may remove him and appoint another in his Stead.

Quorum of Senate

35 Until the Parliament of Canada otherwise provides, the Presence
of at least Fifteen Senators, including the Speaker, shall be necessary
to constitute a Meeting of the Senate for the Exercise of its Powers.

Voting in Senate

36 Questions arising in the Senate shall be decided by a Majority of
Voices, and the Speaker shall in all Cases have a Vote, and when the
Voices are equal the Decision shall be deemed to be in the Negative.

Senators not to sit in House of Commons

39 A Senator shall not be capable of being elected or of sitting or
voting as a Member of the House of Commons.

Money Votes; Royal Assent

Appropriation and Tax Bills

53 Bills for appropriating any Part of the Public Revenue, or for imposing any Tax or Impost, shall originate in the House of Commons.

IX. Miscellaneous Provisions

General

Oath of Allegiance, etc.

128 Every Member of the Senate or House of Commons of Canada shall before taking his Seat therein take and subscribe before the Governor General or some Person authorized by him, and every Member of a Legislative Council or Legislative Assembly of any Province shall before taking his Seat therein take and subscribe before the Lieutenant Governor of the Province or some Person authorize by him, the Oath of Allegiance contained in the Fifth Schedule to this Act; and every Member of the Senate of Canada and every Member of the Legislative Council of Quebec shall also, before taking his Seat therein, take and subscribe before the Governor General, or some Person authorized by him, the Declaration of Qualification contained in the same Schedule.

Use of English and French Languages

133 Either the English or French language may be used by any Person in the Debates of the Houses of the Parliament of Canada and of the Houses of the Legislature of Quebec; and both those Languages shall be used in the respective Records and Journals of those Houses; and either of those Languages may be used by any Person or in any Pleading or Process in or issuing from any Court of Canada established under this Act, or in or from all or any of the Courts of Quebec.

The Acts of the Parliament of Canada and of the Legislature of Quebec shall be printed and published in both those Languages.

Notes

CHAPTER ONE | **What Is the Senate?**

1   Senate of Canada, "Proceedings of the Special Committee on Senate Modernization" *Evidence*, 42-1, Issue No 1 (9 March 2016) at 1:30. During his testimony, David E Smith provides this quote.

2   Manitoba's Upper Chamber was abolished in 1876; New Brunswick's in 1892; Prince Edward Island's in 1893; Nova Scotia's in 1928; and Quebec's in 1968. See Audrey O'Brien & Marc Bosc, eds, *House of Commons Procedure and Practice*, 2d ed (Ottawa: House of Commons, 2009) at Figure 1.1. See also DC Harvey, "The Passing of the Second Chamber in Prince Edward Island"(1922) 1:1 *Report of the Annual Meeting* 22 at 22–31; Charles Paul Hoffman, *The Abolition of the Legislative Council of Nova Scotia, 1925–1928* (Master of Laws Thesis, McGill University Institute of Comparative Law, 2011) [unpublished]; and Edmond Orban, "La fin du bicaméralism au Québec" (1969) 2:3 *Canadian Journal of Political Science* 312 at 312–26.

3   *Constitution Act, 1867* (UK), 30 & 31 Vict, c 3, s 53; *Constitution Act, 1982*, s 47(1) being Schedule B to the *Canada Act 1982* (UK), 1982, c 11.

4   *Reference re Senate Reform*, 2014 SCC 32 at para 1 [*Reference re Senate Reform*].

5   Quoted in FA Kunz, *The Modern Senate of Canada,1925–1963: A Re-appraisal* (Toronto: University of Toronto Press, 1965) at 318.

6   Provincial Parliament of Canada, *Parliamentary Debates on the subject of the Confederation of the British North American Provinces*, 8-3 (8 February 1865) at 88.

7   Quoted in Senator Hugh Segal, "Senate Reform and Democratic Legitimacy: Beyond Stasis" in Jennifer Smith, ed, *The Democratic Dilemma: Reforming the*

Canadian Senate (Montreal & Kingston: McGill-Queen's University Press, Institute of Intergovernmental Relations, 2009) at 182.

8   *House of Commons Debates*, 10-4, vol 1 (20 January 1908) at 1571–72.

9   For other examples of distinguished appointments, see Kunz, above note 5 at 60–61.

10 On 18 October 1929, women became qualified for appointment to the Senate. The change was brought about not through a formal constitutional amendment but by a decision of the United Kingdom's Judicial Committee of the Privy Council. See *Edwards v Attorney-General (Canada)*, [1929] UKPC 86 (the *Persons Case*) and Serge Joyal, ed, *Protecting Canadian Democracy: The Senate You Never Knew* (Montreal & Kingston: McGill-Queen's University Press, 2003) at 291 and 312.

11 See CES Franks, *The Parliament of Canada* (Toronto: University of Toronto Press, 1987) at 188.

12 Cited by Joan Powers Rikerd, "Science" in John Saywell & Donald Forster, eds, *Canadian Annual Review for 1970* (Toronto: University of Toronto,1971) at 477.

13 David C Docherty, "The Canadian Senate: Chamber of Sober Reflection or Loony Cousin Best Not Talked About" (2002) 8:3 *The Journal of Legislative Studies* 27 at 27.

14 Franks, above note 11 at 186.

15 See Robert A Mackay, *The Unreformed Senate of Canada*, rev ed (Toronto: McClelland and Stewart, 1963) at 9.

16 John N Turner, "The Senate of Canada-Political Conundrum" in Robert M Clark, ed, *Canadian Issues: essays in honour of Henry F Angus* (Toronto: Published for the University of British Columbia by the University of Toronto Press, 1961) at 57.

17 Smith, above note 7.

18 Mackay, above note 15.

19 David E Smith, "The Improvement of the Senate by Non-constitutional Means" in Joyal, above note 10 at 229.

20 "Proceedings of the Special Committee on Senate Modernization," above note 1. David E Smith, in his testimony before the Special Senate Committee on Senate Modernization, described the Senate as "a *terra incognita* to most citizens." For a list of articles, monographs, legislation, and caselaw regarding the Senate, see Joyal, above note 10 at 331–50.

21 *Re: Authority of Parliament in relation to the Upper House*, [1980] 1 SCR 54, 102 DLR (3d) 1; *Reference re Senate Reform*, above note 4 at paras 48, 52, 69, 75, 77, 79, and 87–91.

22 Leo Strauss & Joseph Cropsey, *History of Political Philosophy*, 3d ed (Chicago & London: University of Chicago Press, 1987) at 3.

23   Quoted in Sydney D Bailey, ed, *The Future of the House of Lords. A Symposium.* (London: The Hansard Society, 1954) at 21.

24   Janet Ajzenstat, "Bicameralism and Canada's Founders: The Origins of the Canadian Senate" in Joyal, above note 10 at 4. See also Janet Ajzenstat et al, eds, *Canada's Founding Debates*, 2d ed (Toronto: University of Toronto Press, 2003) at Introduction.

CHAPTER TWO | **Second Chambers — Theories and Structures**

1   Quoted in FA Kunz, *The Modern Senate of Canada, 1925–1963: A Reappraisal* (Toronto: University of Toronto Press, 1965) at 4.

2   Senate of Canada, "Proceedings of the Special Senate Committee on Senate Reform" *Evidence*, 39-1, Issue No 1 (6 September 2006). Janet Ajzenstat provides this testimony at the Afternoon Meeting.

3   George H Sabine & Thomas L Thorson, *A History of Political Theory*, 4th ed (Hinsdale, IL: Dryden Press, 1973) at 152–53.

4   See George Tsebelis & Jeannette Money, *Bicameralism* (Cambridge: Cambridge University Press, 1997) at 15; John Adams, *Thoughts on Government: applicable to the present state of the American colonies.: In a letter from a gentleman to his friend* (Philadelphia: John Dunlop, M, DCC, LXXVI, 1776; Ann Arbor, MI: Text Creation Partnership); Thomas Paine, *The Rights of Man: Being An Answer to Mr. Burke's Attack on the French Revolution* (Cambridge: Cambridge University Press, 2012).

5   Mariana Llanos & Detlef Nolte, "Bicameralism in the Americas: Around the Extremes of Symmetry and Incongruence" (2003) 9:3 *The Journal of Legislative Studies* 54 at 60, 61, and 77.

6   See MJC Vile, *Constitutionalism and the Separation of Powers*, 2d ed (Indianapolis: Liberty Fund, Inc, 1998) at 58–82.

7   Quoted in Arihiro Fukuda, *Sovereignty and the Sword: Harrington, Hobbes, and Mixed Government in the English Civil Wars* (Oxford: Clarendon Press, 2004) at 25–26.

8   Tsebelis & Money, above note 4 at 35.

9   John Stuart Mill, "Utilitarianism" in HB Acton, ed, *Utilitarianism, On Liberty, and Considerations on Representative Government* (London: JM Dent & Sons, Everyman's Library, 1991) at 353.

10   Tsebelis & Money, above note 4 at 34.

11   Philip Norton, *Reform of the House of Lords* (Manchester: Manchester University Press, 2017) at 3–12.

12   See Meg Russell, "The Territorial Role of Second Chamber" (2001) 7:1 *The Journal of Legislative Studies* 105.

13 Alexander Hamilton, James Madison & John Jay, *The Federalist Papers* (New York and Scarborough, ON: The New American Library of World Literature, 1961) at 377.

14 Tsebelis & Money, above note 4 at 53; Meg Russell, *The Contemporary House of Lords: Westminster Bicameralism Revived* (Oxford: University of Oxford Press, 2013) at ch 3.

15 Quoted in Tsebelis & Money, above note 4 at 34.

16 One of the first modern theorists to advocate for an elected upper house was James Harrington (1611–1677). See his *The Commonwealth of Oceana and A System of Politics*, ed by JGA Pocock (Cambridge: Cambridge University Press, 1992). For a description of the Australian Senate's popular sovereignty design, see *Odgers' Australian Senate Practice*, 14th ed (Canberra: Australian Government Publishing Service for Department of the Senate, 2020).

17 See Russell, above note 14 at ch 3.

18 *Ibid* at 34. Russell calls the House of Lords "a chamber of paradoxes."

19 *Ibid* at ch 3. For surveys of the upper houses of Spain and Italy see Samuel C Patterson & Anthony Mughan, eds, *Senates: Bicameralism in the Contemporary World* (Columbus: Ohio State University Press, 1999).

20 See "National Parliaments" (2022), online: *Inter-Parliamentary Union* www.ipu.org/national-parliaments and Russell, above note 14 at ch 3.

21 See Russell, above note 14 at Table 3.1.

22 Tsebelis & Money, above note 4 at 47.

23 Arend Lijphart, "Bicameralism: Canadian Senate Reform in Comparative Perspective" in Herman Bakvis & William M Chandler, eds, *Federalism and the Role of the State* (Toronto: University of Toronto Press, 1987) at 103. Belgium's Senate has since undergone several constitutional reforms.

24 *Ibid* at 103.

25 See John Uhr, "Generating Divided Government: The Australian Senate" in Patterson & Mughan, above note 19 at 93–119.

26 See Tsebelis & Money, above note 4 at 53.

CHAPTER THREE | **The Vision of the Fathers**

1 See Janet Ajzenstat "Introduction" in GP Browne, ed, *Documents on the Confederation of British North America* (Montreal & Kingston: McGill-Queen's University Press, Carleton Library Series, 2009) at xiv. Ajzenstat's introduction is new.

2 See Christopher Moore, *Three Weeks in Quebec City: The Meeting That Made Canada* (Toronto: Penguin Canada, 2015).

3   See Donald Creighton, *The Road to Confederation: The Emergence of Canada, 1863–1867* (Toronto: Macmillan of Canada, 1964) at 188; and Janet Ajzenstat, Paul Romney, et al, eds, *Canada's Founding Debates*, 2d ed (Toronto: University of Toronto Press, 2003). Kunz recounts the eye-witness recollections of Sir Allen Aylesworth, who was appointed to the Senate in 1923, and was thirteen years old at the time of Confederation:

> [the] subject of the continuance of a second chamber or upper house was, during the time of Quebec Conference, not only a matter of daily reading in the household from the columns of the Toronto Globe, but was a matter of daily, I might say hourly, discussion between themselves ... and with the neighbours about the farm — in the fields or in the barn, wherever they might be working.

FA Kunz, *The Modern Senate of Canada,1925–1963: A Re-appraisal* (Toronto: University of Toronto Press, 1965) at 317.

4   Creighton, above note 3 at 430.

5   Danielle Pinard, "The Canadian Senate: An Upper House Criticized Yet Condemned to Survive Unchanged?" in Jörg Luther, Paolo Passaglia & Rolando Tarchi, eds, *A World of Second Chambers: Handbook for Constitutional Studies on Bicameralism* (Milan: Giuffrè Editore, 2006) at 460.

6   Moore, above note 2 at 89.

7   Provincial Parliament of Canada, *Parliamentary Debates on the Subject of the Confederation of the British North American Provinces*, 8-3 (8 February 1865) at 88.

8   The Province of Canada had an elected Legislative Council from 1856 to 1866. Prince Edward Island adopted the elective system in 1862. New Brunswick had secured permission from the British government in 1851 to make its Legislative Council elective, but the proposal had been blocked by the Council itself. See Robert A Mackay, *The Unreformed Senate of Canada*, rev ed (Toronto: McClelland and Stewart, 1963) at 30–32. See also Colin Grittner, "Constitutional Conservativism, Anti-Democratic Ideology, and the Elective Principle in British North American Upper Legislative Houses, 1848–1867" in Nikolaj Bijleveld et al, eds, *Reforming Senates: Upper Legislative Houses in North Atlantic Small Powers 1800–Present* (London and New York: Routledge, 2020).

9   See Resolution Nine of the Ninety-Two Resolutions, *Journals of the House of Assembly of Lower Canada*, 14-4 (21 February 1834) at 311.

10 Robert Baldwin, along with Louis Hippolyte Lafontaine, has been described as the "Father of Responsible Government." See John Ralston Saul, *Extraordinary Canadians: Louis-Hippolyte LaFontaine & Robert Baldwin* (Toronto: Penguin Canada, 2012).

11 HD Forbes, ed, *Canadian Political Thought* (Toronto: Oxford University Press, 1985) at 29.

12 Browne, above note 1 at 45. Mackay notes that at Quebec, Prince Edward Island, "alone of all the provinces," pressed for an elective council in the new constitution. Above note 8 at 32.

13 David E Smith, *The Canadian Senate in Bicameral Perspective* (Toronto: University of Toronto Press, 2003) at 79.

14 Colin Grittner, *Privilege at the Polls: Culture, Citizenship, and the Electoral Franchise in Mid-Nineteenth-Century British North America* (PhD thesis, McGill University Department of History and Classical Studies, Faculty of Arts, 2015) [unpublished] at 319.

15 *Province of Canada Assembly Debates* (27 March 1855) at 2470.

16 *Parliamentary Debates on the Subject of the Confederation of the British North American Provinces*, above note 7 at 88.

17 Jennifer Smith, "Canadian Confederation and the Influence of American Federalism" (1988) 21:3 *Canadian Journal of Political Science* 455.

18 See Gerald M Craig, ed, *Lord Durham's Report* (Toronto: McClelland and Stewart, Carleton Library no 1, 1963).

19 Pierre Claude Nolin, "Accommodation as a Canadian Tradition" (2008) 31:2 *Canadian Parliamentary Review* 5 at 5.

20 Bicameral legislatures were established in Nova Scotia in 1758; in Prince Edward Island in 1773; in New Brunswick in 1785; and in Ontario and Quebec in 1791. See Mackay, above note 8 at 18.

21 Craig, above note 18 at 169.

22 Browne, above note 1 at 63.

23 Moore, above note 2 at 81.

24 For selected extracts relating to the Senate from the *Constitution Act, 1867* (UK), 30 & 31 Vict, c 3, s 91, reprinted in RSC 1985, Appendix II, No 5 see Appendix.

25 Mackay, above note 8 at 37.

26 In 1867, the population of the Province of Canada was 3,090,936, while New Brunswick's population was 295,084 and Nova Scotia's 368,781. See Donald J Savoie, *Democracy in Canada: The Disintegration of Our Institutions* (Montreal & Kingston: McGill-Queen's University Press, 2019) at 202. The fastest growing province was Upper Canada, or Ontario.

27 Browne, above note 1 at 67.

28 Mackay, above note 8 at 38. The boundaries of Quebec's twenty-four senatorial districts are described in *An Act respecting the Legislative Council*, Schedule A being Title 1, Cap 1 of *The Consolidated Statutes of Canada*, CSC, 1985, c 1, s 1, and Schedule. These districts were the ones Canada East (Quebec) held in the Legislative Council before Confederation. While the boundaries of the province were later extended to include its present land base, those of the senatorial districts were never adjusted and include only a portion of the southern area of the province. On a strict interpretation of the boundaries, the residents of

the northern part of Quebec, in Nunavik, are formally without representation in the Senate. See Dan Hays, "Renewing the Senate under the Section 44 Amending Formula" (2018) 41:4 *Canadian Parliamentary Review* 13.

29 *Parliamentary Debates on the Subject of the Confederation of the British North American Provinces*, above note 7 at 234.

30 Browne, above note 1 at 211.

31 *Parliamentary Debates on the Subject of the Confederation of the British North American Provinces*, above note 7 at 38.

32 *Ibid* at 2.

33 *Ibid* at 238–39.

34 Vincent Pouliot, "The Constitutionality of Bill C-20" in Jennifer Smith, ed, *The Democratic Dilemma: Reforming the Canadian Senate* (Montreal & Kingston: McGill-Queen's University Press, Institute of Intergovernmental Relations, 2009) at 142.

35 Quoted in Janet Ajzenstat, "Bicameralism and Canada's Founders: The Origins of the Canadian Senate" in Serge Joyal, ed, *Protecting Canadian Democracy: The Senate You Never Knew* (Montreal & Kingston: McGill-Queen's University Press, 2003) at 11.

36 Browne, above note 1 at 212.

37 *Ibid*.

38 Mollie Dunsmuir, *The Senate: Appointments under Section 26 of the Constitution Act, 1867* (Ottawa: Library of Parliament Research Paper, 1990). In 1915, Parliament re-organized western representation in the Senate through a constitutional amendment. Because there were now four divisions instead of three, the number of senators who could be appointed under section 26 became four or eight, rather than three or six.

39 Quoted in Moore, above note 2 at 106.

40 *Parliamentary Debates on the Subject of the Confederation of the British North American Provinces*, above note 7 at 240.

41 *Ibid* at 36.

42 *Ibid* at 90.

43 *Ibid* at 225.

44 Browne, above note 1 at 68.

45 *Parliamentary Debates on the Subject of the Confederation of the British North American Provinces*, above note 7 at 35–37.

CHAPTER FOUR | **The Roles of the Senate in Historical Perspective**

1 Gordon Robertson, *A House Divided: Meech Lake, Senate Reform and the Canadian Union* (Halifax: The Institute for Research on Public Policy, 1989) at 4;

Michael Pitfield, "An Appointed Chamber Will Always Lack Credibility "
(1984) 7:1 *Canadian Parliamentary Review* 12; Paul Thomas, "Comparing the
Lawmaking Roles of the Senate and the House of Commons" in Serge
Joyal, ed, *Protecting Canadian Democracy: The Senate You Never Knew* (Montreal &
Kingston: McGill-Queen's University Press, 2003) at 206.

2 Quoted in Leslie F Seidle, "Senate Reform and the Constitutional Agenda:
Conundrum or Solution?" in Janet Ajzenstat, ed, *Canadian Constitutionalism:
1791–1991* (Ottawa: Canadian Study of Parliament Group, 1991) at 94–95.
Seidle also notes that in 1887, at the first Interprovincial Conference, the
premiers adopted a resolution that half the senators from each province
should be appointed by the provincial government and half by the federal
government, in each case for a limited term.

3 See FA Kunz, *The Modern Senate of Canada, 1925–1963: A Re-appraisal* (Toronto:
University of Toronto Press, 1965) at 323–24.

4 David E Smith, *The Canadian Senate in Bicameral Perspective* (Toronto: University
of Toronto Press, 2003) at 92.

5 Kunz, above note 3 at 317.

6 Robert A Mackay, *The Unreformed Senate of Canada*, rev ed (Toronto: McClelland
and Stewart, 1963) at 51.

7 Smith, above note 4 at 98.

8 Provincial Parliament of Canada, *Parliamentary Debates on the Subject of the
Confederation of the British North American Provinces*, 8-3 (8 February 1865)
at 494. Dunkin believed the proposed upper house structure "to be a very
near approach to the worst system which could be devised in legislation."
Ibid at 495.

9 Pitfield, above note 1 at 12.

10 Donald Savoie, *Democracy in Canada: The Disintegration of Our Institutions*
(Montreal & Kingston: McGill-Queen's University Press, 2019) at 6.

11 Of the 103 appointments made to the Senate by Mr King, 101 were Liberals.
Regarding Mr Bennet's 33 appointments, 32 were Conservatives. Mr St Laurent
made 55 appointments and 51 were Liberals. Under Mr Diefenbaker, only 1 of
his 37 appointments was not a Progressive Conservative. Mr Pearson made 39
appointments and 38 were Liberals. Mr Pierre Trudeau made 81 appointments
and 70 were Liberals. All of Mr Clark's 11 appointments were Progressive
Conservatives. Under Mr Mulroney, only 2 of the 57 appointments were not
Progressive Conservatives. Only 3 of Mr Chretien's 75 appointments were
not Liberals. Mr Martin made 17 appointments and 12 were Liberals. Regarding Mr Harper's 59 appointments, all were Conservatives.

12 Jeremy Waldron, *Political Political Theory: Essays on Institutions* (Cambridge, MA
& London: Harvard University Press, 2016) at 82.

13 Quoted in *ibid* at 82.

14 See *Debates of the Senate*, 30-2, vol 2 (14 October 1977) at 1319–22 (Hon Renaude Lapointe).

15 *Debates of the Senate*, 34-2, vol 2 (28 March 1990) at 1402 (Hon Guy Charbonneau).

16 Janet Ajzenstat, "Bicameralism and Canada's Founders: The Origins of the Canadian Senate" in Joyal, above note 1 at 25.

17 The matter was debated at the 1927 Dominion–Provincial Conference but rejected. The conference concluded: "The British system under which in 1911 the powers of the House of Lords with respect to money and general Bills initiated and passed in the representative Chamber were restricted was discussed at considerable length during the conference … While there was a strong body of opinion in favour of any reforms which might strengthen the general machinery of Parliament there was no attempt on the part of any speaker to minimize the value of a second chamber." See Smith, above note 4 at 93. In 1984, the Mulroney government proposed amending the Constitution to give the Senate a suspensive veto on certain bills, but the amendment was abandoned when Quebec and Manitoba, followed later by Ontario, decided to oppose it. See Savoie, above note 10 at 206–7.

18 Serge Joyal, "Conclusion: The Senate as the Embodiment of the Federal Principles" in Joyal, above note 1 at 303.

19 David E Smith, "A House for the Future: Debating Second Chamber Reform in the United Kingdom," (2000) 35:3 *Government and Opposition* 325 at 336.

20 See Smith, above note 4 at 166.

21 Mackay, above note 6 at 137.

22 Kunz, above note 3 at 312–15.

23 Mackay, above note 6 at 94–99.

24 CES Franks, "Not Dead Yet, But Should It Be Resurrected? The Canadian Senate" in Samuel C Patterson & Anthony Mughan, eds, *Senates: Bicameralism in the Contemporary World* (Columbus: Ohio State University Press, 1999) at 124 and 129.

25 *Debates of the Senate*, 35-2, vol 135, Issue No 33 (19 June 1996) at 747 (Hon Gildas L Molgat).

26 Andrew Heard, *Canadian Constitutional Conventions: The Marriage of Law and Politics* (Toronto: Oxford University Press, 1991) at 94–95.

27 Savoie, above note 10 at 214.

28 Kunz, above note 3 at 186.

29 Thomas, above note 1 at 195.

30 Eugene A Forsey, *How Canadians Govern Themselves*, 10th ed (Ottawa: Library of Parliament, 2020) at 34. Forsey served in the Senate from 1970 to 1979.

CHAPTER FIVE | **The Structure of the Senate**

1   *Constitution Act, 1867,* (UK), 30 & 31 Vict c 3, s 147.

2   See Resolution Ten, found in Provincial Parliament of Canada, *Parliamentary Debates on the Subject of the Confederation of the British North American Provinces,* 8-3 (8 February 1865) at 1; *The Province of British Columbia, Order of Her Majesty in Council admitting British Columbia into the Union,* dated 16 May 1871; *An Act to amend and continue the Act 32- 33 Victoria chapter 3; and to establish and provide for the Government of the Province of Manitoba* (Can), 33 Vict, c 3, s 3; *The Alberta Act* (Can), 1905, 4 &5 Edw VII, c 3, s 4; *The Saskatchewan Act* (Can), 1905, 4 &5 Edw VII, c 42, s 4; *The British North America Act 1915* (UK), 5& 6 Geo V, c 45, s 1 (ii).

3   *Parliamentary Debates on the Subject of the Confederation of the British North American Provinces,* above note 2 at 35.

4   Terms of Union of Newfoundland with Canada, s 4 being Schedule to the *Newfoundland Act, 1949* (UK), 12&13 Geo VI, c 22.

5   See *Constitution Act* (No 1), SC 1975, c 28, s 2(2); *Constitution Act, 1999* (Can), 46 &47 Elizabeth II, c 15, s 43(3).

6   See the Standing Committee on the Internal Economy, Budgets and Administration of Canada of the Senate of Canada, *Senators' Travel Policy* (Ottawa, 2012), online: https://sencanada.ca/Content/SEN/Committee/412/ciba/rep/rep07jun14A-e.pdf and Senate of Canada, *Senators' Office Management Policy* (Ottawa, 2017), s 5.14.2, online: https://sencanada.ca/media/360442/ppd_somp_ext_e.pdf.

7   Senators who were "lifers" could choose if they wished to be grandfathered. The last senator for life, Dr Orville Phillips (PEI), resigned in 1999.

8   Suggestions have been made that section 32 be amended to assure the people and regions of Canada their full Senate representation, for example, that the prime minister propose a name of a Senate candidate within 180 days. See Dan Hays, *Renewing the Senate of Canada: A Two-Phase Proposal, with After Word* (Ottawa, 2007) at 37. Legislation has also been introduced on the issue but has to date been unsuccessful.

9   See "Senate of Canada (Standing Committee on Ethics and Conflict of Interest for Senators)" (nd), online: *Senate of Canada* https://sencanada.ca/en/committees/conf; *Constitution Act, 1867,* above note 1, s 33.

10   See "Indemnities, Salaries and Allowances" (1 April 2021), online: *Parliament of Canada* https://lop.parl.ca/sites/ParlInfo/default/en_CA/People/Salaries.

11   See Philip Laundy, *The Office of Speaker in the Parliaments of the Commonwealth* (London: Quiller Press, 1984) at 10. The Senate Speaker is appointed by the Governor General on the advice of the prime minister and may be removed at any time. There has been much debate over the years about modernizing

the Speaker's selection, including possible election by the Senate itself. Such change would require a constitutional amendment. Non-constitutional change has also been suggested. In 2016, the Special Senate Committee on Senate Modernization recommended the Senate direct the Rules, Procedures, and Rights of Parliament Committee to develop a process by which senators could express their preference for a Speaker by nominating up to five senators for consideration by the prime minister to recommend to the Governor General for appointment. See *Journals of the Senate*, 42-1, Issue 60, The Special Senate Committee on Senate Modernization, "Sixth Report" (5 October 2016) at 817–18 (Hon George J Furey).

12   The Senate recognizes two broad categories of bills: "public bills," which relate to public issues within the competency of federal jurisdiction, and "private bills," which are introduced upon petition and confer special benefits on a specific person or group of persons, including corporations. Public bills can be divided into two groups: government bills that are initiated by the government and can be introduced either in the House of Commons or the Senate, and public bills that are initiated by a senator or a member of the Commons who is not a minister. These latter bills are of two types: "Senate Public Bills" and "Commons Public Bills." See Senate of Canada, *Senate Procedure in Practice* (Ottawa, 2015) at 127–28, online: https://sencanada.ca/media/93509/spip-psep-full-complet-e.pdf.

13   FA Kunz, *The Modern Senate of Canada, 1925–1963: A Re-appraisal* (Toronto: University of Toronto Press, 1965) at 233.

14   For many years, divorce legislation was the monopoly of the Senate. Its involvement was lessened pursuant to the reform of divorce law. The Senate still retains the original divorce files, and certified copies of divorce acts may be obtained from the office of the Senate Law Clerk and Parliamentary Counsel. See *ibid* at 213–20.

15   See Senate of Canada, Senate Committees Directorate, *Activities and Expenditures Annual Report 2019–2020* (Ottawa, 2020) at 3 (Principal Clerk: Blair Armitage).

16   A Paul Pross, "Parliamentary Influence and the Diffusion of Power" (1985) 18:2 *Canadian Journal of Political Science* 235.

17   For a general discussion of the principles of parliamentary procedure, see J Gordon Dubroy's introduction to *Bourinot's Rules of Order: A Manual on the Practices and Usages of the House of Commons of Canada and on Procedure at Public Assemblies, Including Meetings of Shareholders and Directors of Companies, Political Conventions and Other Gatherings*, 2d ed (Toronto: McClelland and Stewart, 1963) at x–xii. Dubroy writes: "Traces of the British system may be noted in the procedure of every democratic legislature in the world."

18   See Senate of Canada, *Companion to the Rules of the Senate of Canada*, 2d ed (Ottawa, 2013) at ch 5.

19   For more information on privilege, see Joseph Maingot, *Parliamentary Privilege in Canada*, 2d ed (Montreal & Kingston: McGill-Queen's University Press, 1997).

CHAPTER SIX | **The Senate at Work: Four Case Studies**

1   David E Smith, *The Canadian Senate in Bicameral Perspective* (Toronto: University of Toronto Press, 2003) at 84.

2   See CES Franks, "Not Dead Yet, But Should It Be Resurrected?" in Samuel C Patterson & Anthony Mughan, eds, *Senates: Bicameralism in the Contemporary World* (Columbus: Ohio State University Press, 1999) at 126–27.

3   "An Act to amend the Parole Act and the Penitentiary Act" *Debates of the Senate*, 33-1, vol 3 (24 July 1986) at 2853 (Hon Guy Charbonneau).

4   *Debates of the Senate*, 33-1, vol 1 (20 February 1985) at 553 (Hon Guy Charbonneau).

5   "Bill C-22, An Act to Amend the Patent Act" 3rd reading, *Debates of the Senate*, 33-2, vol 2 (19 November 1987) at 2224 (Hon Guy Charbonneau).

6   The GST's formal title is the *Excise Tax Act, the Criminal Code, the Customs Act, the Customs Tariff, the Excise Act, the Income Tax Act, the Statistics Act and the Tax Court of Canada Act*, SC 1990, c 45.

7   John Lynch-Staunton, "The Role of the Senate in the Legislative Process" (2000) 23:2 *Canadian Parliamentary Review* 10 at 10.

8   See Senate of Canada, The Special Senate Committee on the Pearson Airport Agreements, *Final Report* (December 1995) (Chair: Finlay MacDonald) at 111–16; and Gary Levy, "Summoning and Swearing of Witnesses: Experience of the Pearson Airport Committee" (1996) 19:1 *Canadian Parliamentary Review* 2 at 4.

9   *Parliament of Canada Act*, RSC 1985, c P-1, ss 10–13.

10   *Manual of Official Procedure of the Government of Canada*, vol 1 (Ottawa,1968) at 27.

11   Correspondence from the Department of Justice Canada to the Clerk of the Special Senate Committee on the Pearson Airport Agreements (16 June 1995).

12   Senate of Canada, "Proceedings of the Special Senate Committee on the Pearson Airport Agreement" *Evidence*, 35-1, Issue 22 (21 September 1995). See the testimony of George Thomson, Deputy Minister of Justice.

13   Smith, above note 1 at 111.

14   See Paul Weinberg, *When Poverty Mattered: Then and Now* (Halifax & Winnipeg: Fernwood Publishing, 2019) at ch 9; and The Honourable David A Croll, "Poverty in Canada" (delivered at The Empire Club of Canada, Toronto, 27

July 1972) in *The Empire Club of Canada Addresses* (Toronto: The Empire Club Foundation, 1972) at 191–204.

15   *Ibid.*

16   *Debates of the Senate*, 28-1, vol 1 (8 October 1968) at 210 (Hon Jean-Paul Deschatelets). Senator Croll would later provide updates to the Senate on the issue of poverty. See, for example, "Poverty in Canada Senate Report on Poverty-Poverty Line Update-1986 Printed as an Appendix," *Debates of the Senate Official Report (Hansard)*, 33-2, vol 3, (27 January 1988) at 2582.

17   Brian O'Neal, *Senate Committees: Role and Effectiveness* (Ottawa: Library of Parliament Research Paper, 1994).

18   See Weinberg, above note 14.

19   *Ibid.*

20   O'Neal, above note 17.

21   FA Kunz, *The Modern Senate of Canada,1925–1963: A Re-appraisal* (Toronto: University of Toronto Press, 1965) at 323.

22   *Debates of the Senate*, 35-2, vol 135, Issue 4 (20 March 1996) at 1530 hrs (Hon Gildas L Molgat).

23   *Debates of the Senate*, 35-2, vol 135, Issue 5 (21 March 1996) at 1540 hrs (Hon Gildas L Molgat).

CHAPTER SEVEN | Reviving Canadian Bicameralism: The Non-partisan, Complementary Senate

1   "Justin Trudeau Statement: 'Senate Is Broken and It Needs to Be Fixed'" *CBC News* (29 January 2014), online: www.cbc.ca/news/politics/justin-trudeau-statement-senate-is-broken-and-needs-to-be-fixed-1.2515374.

2   Senate of Canada, "Proceedings of the Special Committee on Senate Reform" *Evidence*, 39-1, Issue No 2 (7 September 2006) at 2:6. During his testimony, The Right Honourable Stephen Harper provided this quote.

3   For a legislative history of Mr Harper's initiatives see Ajit Singh, "Senate Reform, Provinces and the Constitutional Question" *TheCourt.ca* (13 June 2011), online: www.thecourt.ca/senate-reform-provinces-and-the-constitutional-question.

4   "Proceedings of the Special Senate Committee on Senate Reform," above note 2.

5   J Patrick Boyer, *Our Scandalous Senate* (Toronto: Dundurn Press, 2014) at 9. The auditor general made his report in June 2015. See *Report of the Auditor General of Canada to the Senate of Canada — Senators' Expenses* (Ottawa: Office of the Auditor General of Canada, 2015).

6   CES Franks, *The Parliament of Canada* (Toronto: University of Toronto Press, 1987) at 186.

7   Parliament of Canada, *The Special Joint Committee of the Senate and of the House of Commons on the Constitution of Canada, Final Report* (Joint Chairs: Gildas L Molgat & Mark MacGuigan) (May 1972) at 35.

8   UK, Royal Commission on the Reform of the House of Lords, *A House for the Future* (Cm 4534) (London: The Stationery Office, 2000) at 3:12 & 3:13.

9   *Reference re Senate Reform*, 2014 SCC 32 at para 17 [*Reference re Senate Reform*].

10   *Re: Authority of Parliament in relation to the Upper House*, [1980] 1 SCR 54, 102 DLR (3d) 1.

11   *Reference re Senate Reform*, above note 9 at para 57.

12   *Ibid* at Questions 2 & 3, paras 52, 54, 56, 60, 63, 70, 79, 81, 82, and 88.

13   *Ibid* at para 56.

14   *Ibid* at para 58.

15   *Ibid* at para 48.

16   The Court also determined that the abolition of the Senate required the unanimous consent of the Senate, the House of Commons, and the legislative assemblies of all Canadian provinces. *Ibid* at Questions 5 & 6.

17   Donald J Savoie, *Democracy in Canada: The Disintegration of Our Institutions* (Montreal & Kingston: McGill-Queen's University Press, 2019) at 210.

18   Senator Peter Harder, while government representative in the Senate, described in detail his vision of what a non-partisan, complementary Senate should look like. See V Peter Harder, *Complementarity: The Constitutional Role of the Senate of Canada* (Ottawa, 2018).

19   See "Assessment Criteria" (last modified 8 January 2018), online: *Independent Advisory Board for Senate Appointments (Government of Canada)* www.canada.ca/en/campaign/independent-advisory-board-for-senate-appointments/assessment-criteria.html.

20   Savoie, above note 17 at 209.

21   David E Smith, "The Senate of Canada: Renewed Life to an Original Intent" in Nikolaj Bijleveld et al, eds, *Reforming Senates: Upper Legislative Houses in North Atlantic Small Powers 1800–Present* (London & New York: Routledge, 2020) at ch 5.

22   See "Major Legislative and Special Study Reports by Senate Committees, 1961–2019" (January 2020), online: *Committees and Private Legislation Directorate* https://sencanada.ca/en/committees/about/directorate.

23   Institute for Research on Public Policy, *Renewal of the Canadian Senate: Where to from Here? IRPP Report (February)* (Montreal: Institute for Research on Public Policy, 2019) at 10.

24   *Ibid*.

25 Emmett Macfarlane, *The Renewed Canadian Senate: Organizational Challenges and Relations with the Government.* IRPP Study 71 (Montreal: Institute for Research on Public Policy, 2019) at 4.

26 *Journals of the Senate*, 42-1, Issue 292 (unrevised) (28 May 2019); *Journals of the Senate*, 42-1, Issue 298 (unrevised) (6 June 2019).

27 Smith, above note 21.

28 Institute for Research on Public Policy above note 23 at 14. Efforts have been made to augment the Senate's territorial function. In 2016, the Senate Special Committee on Modernization reported two suggestions: (1) the rules of the Senate be amended "to require standing committees to consider regional impacts in their reports on legislation by way of observations or in the report of subject-matter studies, where significant and prejudicial"; and (2) sufficient funds be made available "for committees to travel to all regions of the country when studying bills with potential regional impacts or when considering issues with potential regional impacts where significant or important." See Senate of Canada, *Senate Modernization: Moving Forward, Report of the Special Senate Committee on Senate Modernization-Part 1* (October 2016) at xv (Chairs: Thomas Johnson McInnis & Serge Joyal).

29 Senate of Canada, "Proceedings of the Special Senate Committee on Senate Reform" *Evidence*, 39-1, Issue No 3 (19 September 2006) at 3:10 (Chair: Daniel Hays).

30 See *Memorandum Regarding Certain of the Functions of the Prime Minister*, Order in Council PC 3374 (25 October 1935). In the United Kingdom, some appointments to the upper house are shared with other party leaders. See "How Members Are Appointed" (2022), online: *House of Lords (UK Parliament)* www.parliament.uk/business/lords/whos-in-the-house-of-lords/ members-and-their-roles/how-members-are-appointed.

CHAPTER EIGHT | **Prospects for Structural Reform**

1 Hugh Segal, "We Have the Technology" (2016) 24:1 *Literary Review of Canada* 22, online: https://reviewcanada.ca/magazine/2016/01/we-have-the-technology.

2 *Reference re Senate Reform*, 2014 SCC 32 at question 1, para 75.

3 *Ibid* at question 4. The Court did note, however,

> a full repeal of s 23(3) would render inoperative the option in s 23(6) for Quebec Senators to fulfill their real property qualification in their respective electoral divisions ... The consent of Quebec's National Assembly is required pursuant to s 43 of the *Constitution Act, 1982.*

4 Dan Hays, *Renewing the Senate of Canada: A Two-Phase Proposal, with After Word* (Ottawa, 2007) at 17.

5 See Dan Hays, "Renewing the Senate under the Section 44 Amending Formula" *Canadian Parliamentary Review* 41:4 (2018) 13 at 14.

6 For the references to the major government and parliamentary proposals during this period, see Jack Stilborn, "Forty Years of Not Reforming the Senate — Taking Stock" in Serge Joyal, ed, *Protecting Canadian Democracy: The Senate You Never Knew* (Montreal & Kingston: McGill-Queen's University Press, 2003) at 31–66.

7 British Columbia, *British Columbia's Constitutional Proposals, Paper No 3: Reform of the Canadian Senate* (Victoria, BC: Queen's Printer, 1978).

8 David E Smith, *The Canadian Senate in Bicameral Perspective* (Toronto: University of Toronto Press, 2003) at 7.

9 See Stilborn, above note 6 at 41–42.

10 Quoted in Smith, above note 8 at 54.

11 A further proposal was made in 2006 by Senators Lowell Murray and Jack Austin. They recommended the twenty-four seats currently representing the Western provinces division be distributed among Manitoba, Saskatchewan, and Alberta, and that British Columbia be made a separate division with an allotment of twelve seats. The two senators felt that British Columbia was clearly a distinct fifth region of Canada and its recognition would not be viewed as offensive. See Gary W O'Brien, "Two Senate Changes Are Long Overdue and Within Reach" (9 October 2019), online: *Policy Options* https://policyoptions.irpp.org/fr/magazines/october-2019/two-senate-changes-are-long-overdue-and-within-reach.

12 *Consensus Report on the Constitution: Charlottetown, August 28, 1992: Final Text (Charlottetown Accord)* (August 1992) at 4.

13 Stilborn, above note 6 at 45.

14 Quoted in *ibid* at 34.

15 *Charlottetown Accord*, above note 12 at 4.

16 Stilborn, above note 6 at 31.

17 Donald J Savoie, *Democracy in Canada: The Disintegration of Our Institutions* (Montreal & Kingston: McGill-Queen's University Press, 2019) at 206.

18 Danielle Pinard, "The Canadian Senate: An Upper House Criticized Yet Condemned to Survive Unchanged?" in Jörg Luther, Paolo Passaglia & Rolando Tarchi, eds, *A World of Second Chambers: Handbook for Constitutional Studies on Bicameralism* (Milan: Giuffrè Editore, 2006) at 459.

19 David E Smith, *Coming to Terms: An Analysis of the Supreme Court Ruling on the Senate, 2014* (2015) at 5, online: https://sencanada.ca/content/sen/committee/421/MDRN/Briefs/MDRN_FINAL-SupremeCourtRulingAnalysis(Prof.DavidSmith)_e.pdf.

20 Bruce M Hicks & André Blais, "Restructuring the Canadian Senate through Elections" (2008) 14:15 *IRPP Choices* 2 at 15. Counter arguments have been made that an elected Senate would strengthen parliamentary government. In 2010, Roger Gibbins and Robert Roach pointed to the positive example of Australia's elected Senate. Quoting from Australian political scientist Dr Campbell Sharman, they write:

> Australian experience demonstrates the considerable benefits in the form of increased responsiveness that flow from an institutional check on the executive dominance of the legislative process. Such a check invigorates the legislature and greatly increases the effectiveness of parliamentary scrutiny of government administration. It counters the distortions of the policy process that flow from the executive's attempts to reduce the influence of rival views of the national interest, to smother informed debate of its policies in the legislature and to avoid the necessity of compromise once a measure has partisan endorsement.

See Roger Gibbins & Robert Roach, *The West in Canada Research Series: A New Senate for a More Democratic Canada* (Calgary: Canada West Foundation, 2010) and Campbell Sharman, *The Australian Triple-E Senate: Lessons for Canadian Senate Reform?* (Calgary: Canada West Foundation, 1989).

21 Gordon Robertson, *Memoirs of a Very Civil Servant: Mackenzie King to Pierre Trudeau* (Toronto: University of Toronto Press, 2000) at 359.

22 David E Smith, above note 8 at 155–56.

23 Jennifer Smith, ed, *The Democratic Dilemma: Reforming the Canadian Senate* (Montreal & Kingston: McGill-Queen's University Press, Institute of Intergovernmental Relations, 2009) at 3.

24 Savoie, above note 17 at 206–7.

25 Ty Ludwig, "Failure at Charlottetown: Why the Accord Broke Down" (31 March 2008), online: *The Wire* http://cantory.blogspot.com/2008/04/failure-at-charlottetown-why-accord.html.

26 Robertson, above note 21 at 359.

27 Senate of Canada, "Proceedings of the Special Senate Committee on Senate Reform" *Evidence*, 39-1, Issue No 4 (20 September 2006). Peter McCormick provides this quote at the Morning Meeting.

28 Meg Russell, *An Appointed Upper House: Lessons from Canada (Constitution Unit Publications 29)* (London: The Constitution Unit, Department of Political Science, UCL, 1998) at 8–9.

29 See Michael Pitfield, "An Appointed Chamber Will Always Lack Credibility" (1984) 7:1 *Canadian Parliamentary Review* 12.

30 Canada, Constitutional Conference (1968), *The Constitution and the People of Canada: An Approach to the Objectives of Confederation, the Rights of People and the Institutions of Government* (Ottawa: Queen's Printer, 1969) at 30.

31 Parliament of Canada, *Final Report of the Special Joint Committee of the Senate and of the House of Commons on the Constitution of Canada* (Joint Chairs: Gildas L Molgat & Mark MacGuigan) (1972) at 34.

32 See Senate of Canada, "Proceedings of the Special Committee on Senate Reform" *Evidence*, 39-1, Issue No 3 (19 September 2006) at 3:25-29. Philip Resnick provides testimony here; and Aaron Hynes, "Toward a Rational Redistribution of Seats in Canada's Senate" (2010) 33:4 *Canadian Parliamentary Review* 27.

33 Senate of Canada, "Proceedings of the Special Senate Committee on Senate Reform" *Evidence*, 39-1, Issue No 1 (6 September 2006) at 1:29. CES (Ned) Franks provides this testimony here.

34 Hays, above note 4 at 25–26.

35 The Beaudoin–Dobbie Joint Committee on the proposed 1991 constitutional amendments applauded the Senate's current investigative role and proposed its continuation in a reformed institution. See *Report of the Special Joint Committee on a Renewed Canada* (Ottawa: 1992) at 43.

36 Stilborn, above note 6 at 55.

Bibliography

AJZENSTAT, JANET, PAUL ROMNEY, IAN GENTLES, AND WILLIAM D GAIRDNER, EDS. *Canada's Founding Debates*, 2d ed (Toronto: University of Toronto Press, 2003).

BROWNE, GP, ED. *Documents on the Confederation of British North America.* New Introduction by Janet Ajzenstat (Montreal & Kingston: McGill-Queen's University Press, Carleton Library Series, 2009).

CAMPION, LORD. "Second Chambers in Theory and Practice" *Parliamentary Affairs*, 7, 1953–54.

CANADA. Legal and Constitutional Affairs Committee. *Report on Certain Aspects of the Canadian Constitution* (Ottawa: Queen's Printer, 1980).

———. Legislature. *Parliamentary Debates on the Subject of the Confederation of the British North American Provinces* (Quebec: Hunter Rose, 1865).

DOCHERTY, DAVID C. "The Canadian Senate: Chamber of Sober Reflection or Loony Cousin Best Not Talked About," *The Journal of Legislative Studies*, 8(3), 2002.

FORSEY, EUGENE A. *How Canadians Govern Themselves*, 10th ed (Ottawa: Library of Parliament, 2020).

FRANKS, CES. *The Parliament of Canada* (Toronto: University of Toronto Press, 1987).

GIBBINS, ROGER & ROBERT ROACH. "A New Senate for a More Democratic Canada," The Canada West Foundation, The West in Canada Research Series, March 2010.

HARDER, V PETER. "Complementarity: The Constitutional Role of the Senate of Canada," Senate of Canada, 2018.

HAYS, DAN. "Renewing the Senate of Canada: A Two-Phase Proposal, with After Word," Senate of Canada, 2007.

———. "Reviving Conference Committees," *Canadian Parliamentary Review*, 31(3) 2008.

———. "Renewing the Senate under the Section 44 Amending Formula," *Canadian Parliamentary Review,* 41(4) 2018.

HEARD, ANDREW. *Canadian Constitutional Conventions: The Marriage of Law and Politics* (Toronto: Oxford University Press, 1991).

HICKS, BRUCE M & ANDRÉ BLAIS. "Restructuring the Canadian Senate through Elections," *IRPP Choices*, 14(15) 2008.

HYNES, AARON. "Toward a Rational Redistribution of Seats in Canada's Senate," *Canadian Parliamentary Review*, 33(4) 2010.

INSTITUTE FOR RESEARCH ON PUBLIC POLICY. Report, *Renewal of the Canadian Senate: Where to from Here?* Montreal: February 2019.

JOYAL, SERGE, ED. *Protecting Canadian Democracy: The Senate You Never Knew* (Montreal & Kingston: McGill-Queen's University Press, 2003).

KUNZ, FA. *The Modern Senate of Canada, 1925–1963: A Re-appraisal* (Toronto: University of Toronto Press, 1965).

LEVY, GARY. "Summoning and Swearing of Witnesses: Experience of the Pearson Airport Committee," *Canadian Parliamentary Review*, 19(1) 1996.

LIJPHART, AREND. "Bicameralism: Canadian Senate Reform in Comparative Perspective." In Herman Bakvis & William M Chandler, eds. *Federalism and the Role of the State* (Toronto: University of Toronto Press, 1987).

LYNCH-STAUNTON, JOHN. "The Role of the Senate in the Legislative Process," *Canadian Parliamentary Review*, 23(2) 2000.

MACKAY, ROBERT A. *The Unreformed Senate of Canada*, rev ed (Toronto: McClelland and Stewart, 1963).

MOORE, CHRISTOPHER. *Three Weeks in Quebec City: The Meeting That Made Canada* (Toronto: Penguin Canada, 2015).

NORTON, PHILIP. *Reform of the House of Lords* (Manchester, UK: Manchester University Press, 2017).

O'BRIEN, GARY WILLIAM. "Discovering the Senate's Fundamental Nature: Moving beyond the Supreme Court's 2014 Opinion," *Canadian Journal of Political Science*, 52(3) 2019.

O'NEAL, BRIAN. *Senate Committees: Role and Effectiveness* (Ottawa: Library of Parliament Research Paper, 1994).

PATTERSON, SAMUEL C & ANTHONY MUGHAN, EDS. *Senates: Bicameralism in the Contemporary World* (Columbus: Ohio State University Press, 1999).

PINARD, DANIELLE. "The Canadian Senate: An Upper House Criticized Yet Condemned to Survive Unchanged?" In Jorg Luther, Paolo Passaglia & Rolando Tarchi, eds. *A World of Second Chambers: Handbook for Constitutional Studies on Bicameralism* (Milan: Giuffrè Editore, 2006).

PITFIELD, MICHAEL. "An Appointed Chamber Will Always Lack Credibility," *Canadian Parliamentary Review*, 7(1) 1984.

PROSS, A PAUL. "Parliamentary Influence and the Diffusion of Power," *Canadian Journal of Political Science*, 18(2) 1985.

ROBERTSON, GORDON. *A House Divided: Meech Lake, Senate Reform and the Canadian Union* (Halifax: The Institute for Research on Public Policy, 1989).

RUSSELL, MEG. *Reforming the House of Lords: Lessons from Overseas* (Oxford: Oxford University Press, 2000).

———. *The Contemporary House of Lords: Westminster Bicameralism Revived* (Oxford: University of Oxford Press, 2013).

———. "The Territorial Role of Second Chamber," *The Journal of Legislative Studies*, 7(1) 2001.

SAVOIE, DONALD J. *Democracy in Canada: The Disintegration of Our Institutions* (Montreal & Kingston: McGill-Queen's University Press, 2019).

SEGAL, HUGH. "The Future of the Senate: How to Rejuvenate a Torpid Chamber," *Literary Review of Canada*, 24(1) 2016.

SMITH, DAVID E. *The Canadian Senate in Bicameral Perspective* (Toronto: University of Toronto Press, 2003).

SMITH, JENNIFER, ED. *The Democratic Dilemma: Reforming the Canadian Senate* (Montreal & Kingston: McGill-Queen's University Press, Institute of Intergovernmental Relations, 2009).

SUPREME COURT OF CANADA. *Reference re Legislative Authority of Parliament in Relation to the Upper House*, [1980] 1 SCR 54.

———. *Reference re Senate Reform*, [2014] 1 SCR 704.

TSEBELIS, GEORGE & JEANNETTE MONEY. *Bicameralism* (Cambridge: Cambridge University Press, 1997).

Index

About the Author

Gary William O'Brien was born in Toronto in 1951. He holds a BA (Honours) degree from Glendon College, York University, and an MA and PhD from Carleton University, all in political science. He studied in Toulouse, France, from 1974–75 and started working in the Parliament of Canada in 1975. He was named Clerk of the Senate and Clerk of the Parliaments in 2009, retiring in February 2015. He has published articles in the *Canadian Journal of Political Science*, the *Canadian Parliamentary Review*, *The Table*, and *Ontario History*. He was President of the Canadian Study of Parliament in 1990 and 1991.

About the Editor

Gregory Tardi, BCL, LLB, DJur, is the general editor of the Understanding Canada Collection. He is a member of the Barreau du Québec and serves both as president of the Institute of Parliamentary and Political Law and as editor of the *Journal of Parliamentary and Political Law*. He has served as legal counsel with Elections Canada and at the House of Commons. He has taught at McGill, York and Queen's universities and is the author of several books, including *The Theory and Practice of Political Law* and *Anatomy of an Election*.

Printed and bound by CPI Group (UK) Ltd, Croydon, CR0 4YY

07/07/2026

14916223-0001